KEEP YOUR
HARD-EARNED
MONEY

KEEP YOUR HARD-EARNED MONEY

Tax-Saving Solutions for the Self-Employed

HENRY AIY'M FELLMAN

POCKET BOOKS

New York   London   Toronto   Sydney   Tokyo   Singapore

In view of the complex, individual, and specific nature of financial matters, this book is not intended to replace legal, accounting, or other professional advice. Laws vary from state to state, and the reader is advised to obtain assistance or advice from a competent professional before making decisions about personal financial matters.

The author and publisher disclaim any responsibility for any liability, loss, or risk incurred as a consequence of the use of this book.

An *Original* Publication of POCKET BOOKS

POCKET BOOKS, a division of Simon & Schuster Inc.
1230 Avenue of the Americas, New York, NY 10020

ISBN: 0-671-01530-3

First Pocket Books trade paperback printing February 1998

10   9   8   7   6   5   4   3   2   1

POCKET and colophon are registered trademarks of
Simon & Schuster Inc.

Cover design by Tai Lam Wong
Front cover illustration by Ron Barrett
Text design by Stanley S. Drate/Folio Graphics Co. Inc.

Printed in the U.S.A.

This book is written for all the hardworking Americans who have set out on their own, in the good ol' American entrepreneur spirit, and are trying to make ends meet—not earning enough money that they can take advantage of the tax loopholes afforded the rich, yet earning too much to avoid paying taxes. Simply put, this book is for the people who bear the brunt of the tax burden.

CONTENTS

KEEPING MORE OF YOUR HARD-EARNED MONEY

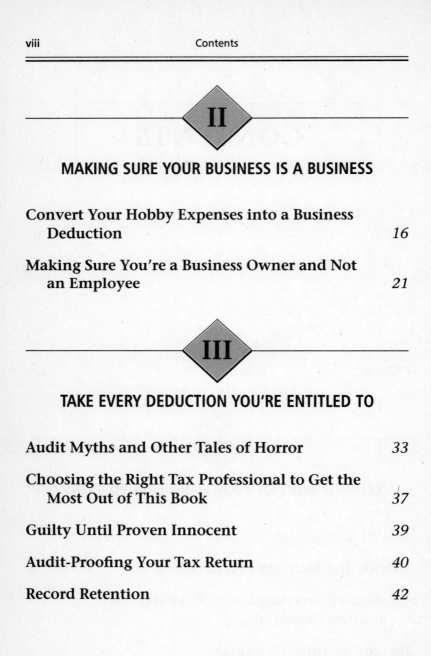

II

MAKING SURE YOUR BUSINESS IS A BUSINESS

III

TAKE EVERY DEDUCTION YOU'RE ENTITLED TO

IV

CONVERTING EVERYDAY LIVING EXPENSES INTO BUSINESS DEDUCTIONS

V

INCOME-SHIFTING TECHNIQUES

VI

RETIREMENT PLANS FOR THE SELF-EMPLOYED

VII

CHOOSING THE FORM OF ENTITY
THAT'S BEST FOR YOU

APPENDICES

PREFACE

Roscoe Egger, Jr., former commissioner of the IRS, has been quoted as stating, "Any tax practitioner, any tax administrator, any taxpayer who has worked with the Internal Revenue Code knows that it is probably the biggest mishmash of statutes imaginable."

As Ronald Reagan is reported to have said, "The government has the nerve to tell the people of the country, 'You figure out how much you owe us, and we can't help you because our people don't understand it either; and if you make a mistake, we'll make you pay a penalty for making the mistake.'"

This process is so complex that Albert Einstein was prompted to say, "The hardest thing in the world to understand is income tax." If it's that difficult for one of the smartest people who ever lived to understand, how is the average taxpayer supposed to use such a system wisely?

It's no wonder most taxpayers—those who can't afford to pay the exorbitant rates charged by most lawyers and CPAs—end up paying far more in taxes than the law requires.

Early in my career, my work at a Big Eight CPA firm included saving lots of money for the very rich. However, after a while I realized that helping them afford a second yacht or another flight to Paris for lunch was not fulfilling to me—which is why I've spent the past 18 years working with small businesses. I've found it much more rewarding and satisfying to help people make enough money to put food on their tables, to keep roofs over their heads, and even to enjoy life.

Recently, I expanded these activities by founding Keep What You Earn!™ and creating affordable, quality workshops and publications to help self-employed people make their small businesses more profitable. This book is part of that effort.

In this book I show self-employed individuals how to take advantage of the tax code and get BIG tax-saving deductions.

All the tax-saving techniques presented are 100% legal. Not only are these techniques absolutely legitimate, but I've presented them in plain, everyday English with easy-to-follow, step-by-step instructions.

It's not enough that we are burdened by a tax law that is already an overly complicated maze of unintelligible rules and regulations, but Congress, The Internal Revenue Service, and the courts also seemingly conspire to keep us in a continuous state of confusion by constantly making new laws, reinterpreting old law, and revising the tax code's regulations. It's almost impossible to keep up with all these changes unless you do it as a full-time job.

That's my job—to help you better understand taxes and make April 15 not a day to dread, but a time to save your money.

KEEPING MORE OF
YOUR HARD-EARNED
MONEY

Do you know your *Tax Bracket?*

When I ask this question at my Keep What You Earn!™ workshops, invariably I'm met with many blank stares. Then I explain, "Your tax bracket is the percent of your next dollar of income that will go to the government. In other words, if the profit from your business is $50,000 for the year, how much of the last dollar you earned for the year do you get to keep?" I get responses ranging from "I don't know" to 70%. Whatever the answer, everyone agrees IT'S TOO MUCH! We all want to keep more of our hard-earned money.

▶ THE #1 TAX SHELTER

Procedures that help us keep more of what we earn are generally called *tax shelters*. Many people think of tax shelters as a means of reducing taxes. However, if that's all they did my job would be easy. I'd just tell you, "Stop working!" Your taxes would be reduced to zero, but you'd have no money. In addition to reducing your taxes, the other essential characteristic of a tax shelter is that it increases your cash flow or wealth.

Contrary to what many people believe, tax shelters are not just for the rich. In fact, if you're your own boss, you're already set up to benefit from the best tax shelter—YOUR BUSINESS.

If you own your own business, you will save thousands of dollars every year by implementing the tax-saving strategies presented throughout this book. You will learn what *every* business owner should know: how to convert everyday living expenses into business deductions; how to shift income from your tax bracket to your children, parents, or friends in lower tax brackets; the best type of retirement plan; and the form of taxable entity that's best for your business (partnership, sole proprietorship, etc.).

Tax Bracket

Depending on where you live, there can be as many as five taxes that need to be considered in computing your tax bracket. They are:

- ▶ Federal income tax
- ▶ State income tax
- ▶ Local income tax
- ▶ Social Security tax
- ▶ Medicare tax

An income tax is a tax that is based on income you received throughout the year. The source of income can be derived from active pursuits, such as compensation received as an employee or profits from your business. It can also be from passive sources, such as investments from which you derive interest, dividends, or profits from their sale.

The **federal income tax** is a graduated tax that increases incrementally. That is, as your income gets higher, the tax rate increases. However, when you go into a higher tax bracket, you don't pay the higher rate on all your income—just on the amount over the lower tax bracket.

For example, if in 1996 you filed as "married filing jointly," and your taxable income was $60,000, your total tax would have been $11,587. This tax is computed as follows: the first $40,100 is taxed at 15%, resulting in a tax of $6,015; and the next $19,900 is taxed at the 28% rate, resulting in a tax of $5,572. Although the composite federal income-tax rate is 19.3% ($11,587 divided by $60,000), the federal income-tax bracket is 28%. That's because 28% of your last dollar earned for the year went to the IRS for the federal income tax. Refer to the tax-rate schedule in Appendix A, which shows the federal tax brackets for each different filing status.

State and local income taxes vary from area to area.

Some states, like Washington, Texas, and Florida do not have an income tax. Others have a graduated tax, and some have a flat tax. Only a few local governments, like New York City, have an income tax.

State income taxes are either a graduated incremental tax, such as the federal income tax, or a flat tax. As described above, a graduated incremental income tax imposes different rates of taxation on different levels of income. On the other hand, a flat tax imposes the same rate on all taxable income. If the tax rate is 5%, then every dollar of taxable income you have will be subject to a 5% tax. If your taxable income is $1,000, the tax will be $50. If your taxable income is $1,000,000, the tax will be $50,000.

Social Security and Medicare taxes. Earned income, whether in the form of wages or profits from sole proprietorships or partnerships, is subject to Social Security and Medicare taxes. When applied to wages, these taxes are referred to as FICA (Federal Insurance Contribution Act). When applied to profits from a sole proprietorship or partnership they are called the self-employment tax. The Social Security tax is 12.4% of earned income. However, this tax is limited to the first $65,400 (for 1997) earned during the year. The Medicare tax is 2.9% of earned income; however, there is no upper limit.

For employees, half of the total FICA tax is paid by the employer and half comes out of their paycheck. The self-employment tax is borne totally by the business owners. However, these business owners are entitled to take a deduction that reduces their taxable income to one-half of the self-employment tax liability. After taking into account the tax savings produced by this deduction, the effective self-employment tax is approximately 13% of the first $65,400 (for 1997) of earned income, and 2.5 percent of each dollar of profit in excess of $65,400.*

▶ CALCULATING YOUR TAX BRACKET

Special thanks to Uncle Sammy and Aunt Iris for allowing me to use their real-life situation to illustrate the strategies presented throughout this book.

Here's how Uncle Sammy calculated his tax bracket. Uncle Sammy and Aunt Iris live in Boulder, Colorado. Their sole income is derived from Uncle Sammy's tax-preparation business. They file a joint tax return with taxable income of $60,000. By looking at the Tax Rate Schedule in Appendix A, Sammy determined that his federal income tax rate is 28%. Colorado has a 5% flat tax, and there are no local taxes in Boulder. Adding his income-tax rates with the self-employment tax of 13%, Sammy determines his tax bracket to be 46%. What's your tax bracket? (To find out the tax rates in your state or locale, contact your state's Department of Revenue or a local professional tax preparer.)

---

*Throughout this book are fill-in-the-blank charts that enable you to compute your savings from employing a particular tax-savings technique. In these charts the self-employment tax rate will be assumed to be 13%. However, if your earned income exceeds the Social Security tax cap ($65,400 for 1997), then the self-employment tax should be reduced to 2.5% for the amount exceeding the cap.

SAMMY'S TAX BRACKET

Federal Income-Tax Rate	28%
State Income-Tax Rate	5%
Local Income-Tax Rate	0
Total Income-Tax Rate	33%
Self-Employment Tax Rate	13%
TAX BRACKET	**46%**

CALCULATE YOUR TAX BRACKET

Federal Income-Tax Rate	_____
State Income-Tax Rate	_____
Local Income-Tax Rate	_____
Total Income-Tax Rate	_____
Self-Employment/FICA Rate	_____
TAX BRACKET	_____

▶ CONVERTING EVERYDAY LIVING EXPENSES INTO BUSINESS DEDUCTIONS

When you buy something, when does it cost less than what you pay? (This is not a Zen koan.)

The primary reason owning your own business is a great way to shelter your income from taxes is that you're able to convert everyday living expenses into business deductions. The resulting saving in taxes is like receiving a discount or rebate on everything you buy. This tax savings, discount, or rebate—depending how you look at it—is calculated by multiplying your tax bracket by the purchase price. For example, let's say your tax bracket is 46%. If you purchase $100 of computer supplies to be used for non-business purposes, you pay $100 and it costs you $100. However, if the supplies were for your business, then although you paid $100, your actual cost is only $54.

1. Purchase Price	$100
2. Tax Bracket	46%
3. Tax Savings (Line 1 × Line 2)	$ 46
4. Actual Cost (Line 1 − Line 3)	$ 54

Your goal is to convert as many of your everyday living expenses into business deductions as possible. And as you'll learn in Part Four, when you own your own business, just about everything you do, everywhere you go, and everyone you meet is related to your business. And all expenses related to those activities are deductible.

EXAMPLE

Before Uncle Sammy went into business for himself, he worked for Blockhead Tax Services. His gross annual wages were $60,000. Aunt Iris, having her hands full taking care of the children and the household, did not have any earned income. Of Uncle Sammy's $60,000 of wages, $13,605 went to taxes (see chart below for breakdown of how much money went to each tax). An additional $48,000 was used to pay for the family's costs of living for the year, such as house-related expenses, food, clothing, medical care, dental care, telephone bills, and entertainment. After paying for these taxes and expenses, Sammy was in the red by $1,605 by year's end.

In order to help make ends meet, Uncle Sammy considered quitting his job and starting a tax-preparation business operating out of his home. He figured his business would bring in as much money ($60,000) as he was earning as an employee. That is, gross revenues of $70,000, minus $10,000 in additional expenses incurred for the business. He also calculated that his family's cost of living, $48,000,

	Working as Employee	Self-Employed
Gross Wages/Income	$ 60,000	$ 70,000
Extra Expenses Incurred by the Business		10,000
Total Income Generated	$ 60,000	$ 60,000
Non-converted Everyday Living Expenses	$ 48,000	24,000
Converted Everyday Living Expenses		24,000
Social Security and Medicare Taxes	4,590	5,087
Federal Income Tax	6,862	2,486
State Income Tax	2,153	828
Total Expenditures	$ 61,605	$ 56,401
Cash Flow for Year	$ (1,605)	$ 3,599

would remain the same. However, the difference between working as an employee and being in business for himself is that by being self-employed, Sammy is able to write off half of his $48,000 living expenses as a business deduction. From the chart below, you can see why he decided to go into business for himself. On top of gaining more freedom and control over his life, reducing the time wasted commuting to and from work, and having more time with his loved ones, he has an extra $5,204 for his family by the end of the year.

▶ INCOME-SHIFTING TECHNIQUES

Another great way to reduce your tax bite is by employing the income-shifting techniques discussed in Part Five. With these techniques, you will be able to shift income that would be taxed at your higher tax bracket to someone else who's in a lower tax bracket and so will pay less of it in taxes. Most typically that someone else is your child, though it could be a parent, friend, or other relative.

Here's how it works: Uncle Sammy paid his son Fred $4,000 for office work during 1996. These wages are a business deduction for Sammy, reducing his business' profit by $4,000. Since Sammy's tax bracket is 46%, he received a tax savings of $1,840 ($4,000 × 46%). On the other hand, the $4,000 is income to Fred. However, as you will learn in Part Five, since Fred is under 18 years old, working for one of his parents, and his income is not greater than $4,000, his salary will not be subject to any tax at all! That means their family ends up with an extra $1,840.

Hiring others is just one of the ways to shift income so it's taxed at a lower rate. In Part Five other techniques—such as gift/leaseback, sale/leaseback, and gifting stock—are also presented.

▶ OTHER TAX-SAVING TECHNIQUES

Converting everyday living expenses and income shifting are the two devices that make owning your own business the great tax shelter it is. However, there are also other ways self-employed business owners can use the tax law to reduce their taxes. Parts Six and Seven explore what to consider in choosing a retirement plan and form of entity.

▶ REDUCE INCOME TAXES WITH A SIDELINE BUSINESS

Many people are not in the position to quit their job and go into business for themselves. You don't need to. You can still reap the tax-savings benefits afforded self-employed business owners even if your business is part-time or just a sideline. In fact, why not turn something you enjoy, like a hobby, into a business?

EXAMPLES

Let's say Uncle Sammy decided to continue working for Blockhead and, in addition, started a small tax-preparation business on the side to earn extra money. The chart below reflects the effect that each of four different situations has on Uncle Sammy's cash flow for the year. Notice that in all four situations, Uncle Sammy's wages and the FICA taxes withheld from his Blockhead wages remain the same: $60,000 and $4,590, respectively. Also, in all four situations the total living expenses remain the same, $48,000. However, once Sammy begins his business, he's able to convert $14,000 of the everyday living expenses into business deductions.

Situation #1 reflects the situation Sammy's in if he stays in his job without doing anything else. He's in the red $1,605!

In **Situation #2**, Sammy doesn't generate any extra income from the business itself. The business takes in $10,000 but incurs additional expenses of $10,000. However, by being in business, he is able to convert $14,000 of otherwise nondeductible everyday living expenses into business deductions. This produces a tax savings of $3,193.

Situation #3 shows the business able to generate gross revenues of $15,000, offset by additional expenses of $12,000, thus increasing Sammy's cash flow by $3,000. However, after taking into account the tax savings resulting from converting the everyday living expenses into business deductions, Sammy comes out $5,593 better than he would have, had his sole source of income been Blockhead.

	Wages & No Business: Hypothetical 1	Wages & Business: Hypothetical 2	Wages & Business: Hypothetical 3	Wages & Business: Hypothetical 4
Monies coming in:				
Wages	$ 60,000	$ 60,000	$ 60,000	$ 60,000
Profit from Business (before deducting convertible living expenses)	–0–	–0–	3,000	15,000
Total monies in	$ 60,000	$ 60,000	$ 63,000	$ 75,000
Monies going out: Living Expenses:				
Non-convertible	$ 48,000	$ 34,000	$ 34,000	$ 34,000
Convertible	0	14,000	14,000	14,000
Total Living Expenses	$ 48,000	$ 48,000	$ 48,000	$ 48,000
Taxes: FICA on Sammy's Wages	$ 4,590	$ 4,590	$ 4,590	$ 4,590
Self-Employment Tax on Sammy's Business	0	0	0	141
Federal Income Tax	6,862	4,369	4,819	7,114
State Income Tax	2,153	1,453	1,603	2,203
Total Income-Related Taxes	$ 13,605	$ 10,412	$ 11,012	$ 14,048
Total Monies Out	$ 61,605	$ 58,412	$ 59,012	$ 62,048
Cash Flow for Year	$ (1,605)	$ 1,588	$ 3,988	$ 12,952

In **Situation #4**, Sammy's sideline business does really well. Before taking into account the expenses converted from non-deductible to deductible, he realizes a gain of $15,000 from the business alone. Now, Sammy and his family are $12,952 in the black. Compare Situation #1 with Situation #4. The total taxes related to income in Situation #1 are $13,605, compared with Situation #4's of $14,048. That means the extra $15,000 generated by the business is, instead of being taxed at 46%, being taxed at only 3%.

I've heard many people in need of extra money complain that it doesn't pay for them to get a second job or for their unemployed spouse to even bother looking for a job. "What's the point?" they lament, "Most of it will go to the government anyhow." That's true, *if* you work for someone else. Had Sammy taken a second job instead of starting his own business, their partner, the government, would get 40.65% of every extra dollar earned. However, when he works for himself, the government's take is reduced to 3%.

Turn Your Hobby into a Business

Look what happens if Uncle Sammy, instead of starting a tax-preparation business, turned his expensive hobby, photography, into a business. It seems every year Sammy's buying some kind of new equipment and he's taking more and more film, which needs to be processed. All this adds up. In fact, of the $48,000 living expenses, $5,000 is spent on his photography hobby. Normally this would not be a deductible expense. However, if he turns this hobby into a business, he'll be able to convert those expenses into business deductions. In Sammy's case, since his tax bracket is 46%, the resulting tax savings, discount, or rebate (depending on how you look at it) will be as much as $2,300 of the $5,000.

As you can see, there are great benefits to being your own boss. But you must be careful. To take advantage of the benefits afforded the self-employed you have to make sure your business is really a business in the eyes of the IRS.

II

MAKING SURE
YOUR BUSINESS
IS A BUSINESS

As we discovered in Part I, owning your own business can result in huge tax savings. That's why the IRS doesn't encourage it. Your gain is their loss. So you need to make sure your activity qualifies to be treated as a business instead of just a hobby. Hobbies do not get to take advantage of all the tax savings afforded businesses. Also, independent contractors are considered self-employed and are treated as self-employed business owners, but employees are not. Make sure you really are an independent contractor and not an employee.

> ► **CONVERT YOUR HOBBY EXPENSES INTO A
> BUSINESS DEDUCTION**

The IRS doesn't want you to be able to deduct the cost of doing what you like to do. If your business is perceived by the IRS as a hobby, you'll lose many of the tax benefits afforded business owners. According to the IRS, if you have fun doing what you're doing, it must be a hobby and not a business. Fortunately, in the legal case *Wilson v. Eisner,* and in several subsequent cases, the federal courts held otherwise:

> business will not be turned into a hobby merely because the owner finds it pleasurable; suffering has never been made a prerequisite to deductibility . . . Success in business is largely obtained by pleasurable interest therein.

The Three-Out-of-Five Rule

What distinguishes a business from a hobby? In order for an activity to be considered a business, your purpose for engaging in it must be to make a profit. If you can't show a profit motive, the IRS will classify the activity as a hobby.

If the activity shows a profit for three out of the last five years, it will be presumed to be a business. On the other hand, if the activity shows a loss for three out of the last five years, it will be presumed a hobby. In either case, the presumption is rebuttable. That is, even if the activity shows a loss in all five years, it will still be treated as a business *if* you can demonstrate you operated it as a business.

Likewise, if the activity shows a profit in three out of the last five years, it will be treated as a hobby *if* the IRS can prove you didn't operate it as a business.

Here's what you lose if your activity is classified as a hobby instead of a business:

- ► Losses cannot be used to offset other income.
- ► Many everyday living expenses that are convertible into business deductions cannot be used as a tax deduction.
- ► The home-office deduction is not allowed.
- ► Expenses are deductible only if you itemize deductions on Schedule A of your individual income tax return, and even then the deduction could be limited to the amount that those items exceed 2% of your adjusted gross income.

Showing a profit for three out of five years is not a safe harbor. Don't forget, the presumption created is rebuttable. If the IRS can demonstrate a lack of intent to make a profit, your activity will be classified a hobby. So if your activity shows a $20,000 loss in each of the first two years, don't expect a small profit in each of the next three years to save you from the IRS's scrutiny.

Turning Losses into Profits

There are legitimate ways to turn losses from your business into gains. Many large corporations whose stock is traded over-the-counter do it all the time in order to bolster the value of the stock. Some of the simpler strategies available are:

- ▶ At the end of the year, deferring deductions and accelerating income
- ▶ Not converting otherwise-convertible living expenses into business deductions
- ▶ Disqualifying yourself from being eligible for the home-office deduction

How to Make Sure Your Business Is a Business

There are nine major factors considered in determining whether an activity is engaged in for profit, and therefore a business, or not engaged in for profit, and therefore a hobby. Satisfying the following guidelines helps demonstrate a profit motive. Keep in mind, these are only for guidance. You don't have to satisfy all to be considered "in business."

1. Conduct your activity in a businesslike manner:
   - ▶ Keep accurate and separate books and records
   - ▶ Have business cards and stationery with your letterhead
   - ▶ Have a separate bank account for your business
   - ▶ Obtain necessary licenses
   - ▶ Obtain a Federal Employee Identification Number (Form SS-4)
   - ▶ Promote your business
   - ▶ Use an appointment book

2. Have proof that you or your advisers have the knowledge and expertise to run a successful business:
   - ▶ Take training seminars, workshops, and classes

> ▶ Acquire publications related to your business
> ▶ Hire competent business advisers

3. Be able to show that you put time and energy into your business. One way to show this is by including in your appointment book all the places you went to and people you met with in regards to your business.

4. Even if your business loses money, its assets may be appreciating in value. For example, if you lease classic automobiles that are increasing in value, the expected gains from the cars might offset the losses from your day-to-day operations and so the activity would be classified as a business.

5. Show a successful track record in carrying on prior business activities. If this is not your first attempt in business, and you've been successful in other business ventures, that will be an additional indication that your current activity is not a hobby.

6. Show a profitable history in this particular activity. If you've been operating this business for—let's say— ten years, and all but the last three years have been profitable, it is more than likely that the activity will be considered a business.

7. Show that occasional profits in this activity more than offset its losses. Let's say your business lost money in three out of its five years in operation. However, the two years of profit total more than the combined three years of losses. In that case, the activity will probably be considered a business.

8. Have no substantial income elsewhere. In Uncle Sammy's and Aunt Iris's situation it was Sammy's photography hobby that was converted into a business. However, since he already had a substantial income from another source and Aunt Iris was unemployed, it would have been better for Aunt Iris to have owned the business.

9. Demonstrate it's something you're doing for money, not just for personal pleasure or recreation. The IRS doesn't believe you can have fun while working. However, remember the quote at the beginning of Part Four? The federal courts do. But you need to document financial motives as well. For example, if you're a photographer, keep a log of all the places you displayed your work, all the places you went to, and all the people you attempted to sell your photographs to.

Form 5213

The IRS doesn't always try to hurt us. Sometimes they try to help us out. By filing Form 5213, "Election to Postpone Determination as to Whether the Presumption That an Activity is Engaged in for Profit Applies," you can elect for the IRS not to determine whether your activity is a hobby or business until after the first five years of operations. Many businesses don't start showing a profit until after their first two or three years in business. By filing this form, you're ensuring yourself that the IRS won't determine whether your activity is a hobby or business until after its fifth year, when a profit is more likely.

Sound good? There are two major drawbacks to filing this form. One is, you're ratting on yourself and increasing your chances of being audited. The second is, by filing this form you're agreeing to extend the IRS's three-year statute of limitations (to audit the year in question) to five years.

Prime Targeted Activities

The following are the activities the IRS loves to claim are really hobbies and not businesses:

► Writing
► Photography
► Painting

► **MAKING SURE YOU'RE A BUSINESS OWNER AND NOT AN EMPLOYEE**

ATTENTION! Independent contractors and hirers classifying workers as independent contractors, the IRS wants YOU!

According to the IRS, the federal government is losing six billion dollars every year due to misclassifying workers. Workers classified as independent contractors are treated as business owners for tax purposes, and so their hirers are not liable for payroll taxes. If the same worker is classified as an employee, the government collects much more in payroll taxes from the employer and income taxes from the worker. In order to minimize these lost revenues, the IRS has a special department whose sole task is to find workers misclassified as independent contractors instead of as employees.

Benefits of Being an Independent Contractor

For most workers it is more beneficial to be classified as an independent contractor than as an employee. By being an independent contractor you're able to:

- ▶ **Reduce** the taxable amount of the gross income you receive by taking advantage of all the tax-saving benefits afforded the self-employed.
- ▶ **Increase** your take-home pay, since taxes are not withheld from your paycheck.
- ▶ **Enjoy** more freedom to do what you want, when you want to do it, and with whom you want to do it.

However, being an independent contractor is like a bed of roses: it looks attractive and smells good, but there are some thorns. As an independent contractor you are not entitled to the fringe benefits afforded employees working for the same company, even if they're doing the same job as you. Also, employers pay half of their employees' Social Security and Medicare taxes, but as an independent contractor you're responsible for the entire 15.3%—though you do get a deduction for half those taxes.

Benefits for Hiring Independent Contractors

Employers almost always benefit when they hire workers as independent contractors as opposed to as employees. Here are some of the benefits:

▶ **Eliminate payroll taxes.** Hirers of independent contractors are not liable for Social Security and Medicare taxes, federal unemployment insurance, or state unemployment insurance. These savings amount to about 12% of the worker's pay.

▶ **Eliminate workers' compensation.** The rate for workers' compensation varies from state to state and occupation to occupation. For example, in many states, employers of construction workers might have to pay more than 30% on an employee's first $15,000 of income, whereas workman's compensation for office workers can be less than 1% of wages paid.

▶ **Reduce costly fringe benefits.** Employers providing fringe benefits need only do so for employees, not for independent contractors. Such benefits include retirement plans, health insurance, medical and dental reimbursement plans, and paid vacations, holidays, and sick leave.

▶ **Reduce record-keeping costs.** It's much more costly to maintain records on employees than on independent contractors. For the latter, the employer only needs to issue checks and submit Form 1099 at the end of the year. However, for each employee the employer needs, at the least, to calculate withholding taxes, to make monthly withholding deposits, to file quarterly and annual forms for withholding, and to pay for unemployment insurance and workman's compensation. In addition, employers are responsible for providing W-2s to the employee, state, and IRS.

All in all, these employee-related expenses, on the average, cost employers an additional 20%–40% of gross pay. So let's say you hire two workers to do the same job. They each get paid $100. However, one is hired as an employee and the other as an independent contractor. The employee might actually cost you $120–$140, while the independent contractor costs you only $100.

When in Doubt, Play It Safe!

With all the additional costs of hiring workers as employees, it's no wonder employers often insist on workers being classified as independent contractors. However, it's also not a great surprise to learn that the IRS nails many employers on this misclassification issue—and the major way is by the companies' competitors ratting on them. If you're hiring workers as employees, while your competition is hiring workers doing the same work as independent contractors, how are you going to compete with them? Your costs are going to be much higher and you'll have to charge more for the same service. You'll be out of business unless you also pay your workers as independent contractors, or you call the IRS and rat on your competition.

Other common causes of worker-classification audits include:

▶ The worker being audited because he or she received only one 1099

▶ The worker claiming unemployment benefits

▶ A random audit by the IRS, Worker's Compensation, or State Unemployment Insurance

The Dangers of Misclassification

As you'll learn in the next section, one tax-saving rule of thumb is, "When in doubt, deduct!" However, this principle does not apply to the issue of worker classification. If you're unsure whether workers are employees or independent contractors, play it safe and hire them as employees. There's too much at stake. If you do get audited for this issue and the IRS determines that you misclassified your workers, you will be subject to back taxes, interest, and very stiff penalties.

In addition to the employer's share of payroll taxes, there's an added penalty of 1.5% of the worker's wages *plus* 20% of the worker's share of Social Security and Medicare taxes. And if you didn't file Form 1099-Misc for the money received by the worker, the penalty doubles. For example, if you paid a worker $20,000 as an independent contractor, and that worker gets reclassified as an employee, you'll end up owing the IRS $5830. And if you didn't file Form 1099-Misc you would owe $11,660.

The Primary Determining Factor: *CONTROL*

There is a common misconception that if someone doesn't work at least a certain number of hours or doesn't make at least $600 throughout the year, that worker does not have to be classified as an employee. Unfortunately, this is not the case. In fact, technically speaking, if someone works for you just a couple of hours and only receives minimum wage, that might still be an employee. It's not how long they work or how much they get paid.

Rather, the most significant factor is one of **CONTROL.** If the employer has the *right* to control and direct the worker, then the worker is an employee. In other words, if the hirer has the right to control what will be done, how it will be done, when it will be done, and where it will be done, the worker is an employee.

The word "right" is emphasized because even if the employer doesn't exercise the right, as long as he has the power, the worker is an employee.

A Rose by Any Other Name Is Still a Rose Just the Same

Another common misconception is the belief that if the hirer and the worker agreed that the worker would be an independent contractor, the IRS will not challenge that classification. This is not true. Regardless of what the worker and hirer agree, if the worker smells like an employee, looks like an employee, and acts like an employee, he or she will be treated as an employee by the IRS.

Listed below are twenty factors that will help you determine the status of a worker. If you're the hirer, bear in mind what happened to Microsoft. Microsoft and some of their workers agreed to enter into an independent-contractor arrangement. However, the IRS reclassified these workers as employees, and Microsoft got nailed with huge back taxes, interest, and penalties. Then the reclassified workers sued Microsoft, claiming that since the court determined them to be employees they were entitled to the fringe benefits afforded other Microsoft employees. In 1996 the court agreed, and unless the initial court's ruling is overturned, it will cost Microsoft a lot more money (*Viscaino v. Microsoft Corp*).

The 20 Factors

The following list of twenty factors, supplied by the IRS, can be used to help you determine the status of a worker. The degree of importance of each factor varies, depending on the type of work performed and the factual context in which the services are performed. This is just a guide; it will not give you a definitive answer.

THE 20 FACTORS

For the following 17 questions a "NO" puts a ✔ in the independent contractor column.

	YES	NO
1. Must the worker comply with the employer's instructions about when, where, or how to work?	☐	☐
2. Does the worker receive employer-sponsored training?	☐	☐
3. Does the worker provide services that are an integral part of the business?	☐	☐
4. Must the worker render services personally?	☐	☐
5. Does the worker hire, supervise, and pay assistants for the employer?	☐	☐
6. Does the worker have a continuing relationship with the employer?	☐	☐
7. Must the worker follow set hours of work?	☐	☐
8. Does the worker work full time for the employer?	☐	☐
9. Does the worker work on the employer's premises?	☐	☐
10. Does the worker perform tasks in an order of sequence set by the employer?	☐	☐
11. Must the worker submit oral or written reports?	☐	☐
12. Is the worker paid by hour, week, or month?	☐	☐
13. Is the worker paid for business and/or travelling expenses?	☐	☐
14. Is the worker furnished by the employer with tools and materials?	☐	☐
15. Does the worker work for only one employer at a time, and not have a risk of loss?	☐	☐
16. Can the worker be fired, other than for breach of contract?	☐	☐

17. May the worker quit without incurring liability to the employer? ☐ ☐

For the following 3 questions, "YES" puts a ✔ in the independent contractor column.

18. Does the worker have a significant investment in the service-provided facilities? ☐ ☐

19. Can the worker realize a profit or loss? Potential risk of loss is a big factor. ☐ ☐

20. Does the worker make his or her services available to the general public? ☐ ☐

How to Make Sure a Worker Is Classified as an Independent Contractor

If you treat someone as an independent contractor, you should:

▶ Have a solid written agreement (please see Appendix B).

▶ Keep to the terms of the agreement

▶ Make sure the worker operates like a business (For example, the worker should have business cards, invoices, a separate office, letterhead stationery, a business license, a business phone and listing, etc).

▶ If the worker's business is incorporated, include "Inc." at the end of payee's name on the check and in your check register

▶ Treat the worker as a business

▶ File the necessary papers (such as Form 1099-MISC)

▶ Not dictate working hours. Setting deadlines are okay.

▶ Not supply cars and equipment; the workers should supply their own

The worker should:

▶ Operate as a business, having business cards, invoices, a separate office, letterhead stationery, a business license, and a business phone and listing
▶ Incorporate, if possible
▶ Work on his or her own premises
▶ Bill you for services rendered
▶ Be paid on project basis instead of receiving a weekly fee, or by the job instead of the hour
▶ Keep his or her own separate accounting records
▶ Work for others, so that the worker doesn't receive just one Form 1099-MISC.

When Is a Rose Not a Rose?

The different branches of government have different definitions for employees and independent contractors. A worker could be classified as an independent contractor for income-tax purposes and an employee for Social Security purposes.

Statutory Employees. The following workers are always classified as employees for FICA purposes. However, they may be treated as self-employed for purposes of deducting business-related expenses on their sole-proprietor business tax return (Schedule C).

▶ Corporate officers who provide services to their corporation

▶ Drivers delivering food, other than milk, to retailers, laundry, or other similiar businesses

▶ Full time, business-to-business salespeople. Example: Manufacturers' representatives

▶ Full time life-insurance agents working mostly for one company

▶ Home workers who do piecework (such as quilts, buttons, gloves, and clothing) according to specifications and out of material supplied by the hirer

Statutory Non-Employees. Some workers are statutorily considered non-employees, such as real estate salespersons and direct sellers of consumer products who sell other than at retail stores or showrooms. To fit within this category, these workers' incomes must be determined by sales, not by the number of hours they worked.

The Safe Harbor

If you have erroneously classified a worker as an independent contractor, you will not have to worry about the past, and you will not even have to make the change for the future *if:*

1. You had a *reasonable basis* for treating the worker as an independent contractor, *and;*
2. All the required federal information and employment-tax forms that you filed are consistent with this basis, *and;*
3. You haven't treated any worker holding a similar position as an employee since the beginning of 1978.

Any of the following three grounds can be relied upon to satisfy the *"reasonable basis"* criterion:

- ▶ Judicial precedent
- ▶ IRS precedent, or
- ▶ More than 25% of the companies in your industry follow the practice of hiring workers as independent contractors

However, it should be noted that these safe-harbor provisions apply only to the IRS, not to state agencies. Also, these safe-harbor provisions do not apply to technical service specialists, such as engineers, designers, programmers, and system analysts.

▶ **HELP!** *Are all these rules and considerations leaving you more unsure than when you started? You can relieve yourself of the burden of figuring out how to classify your workers by filing Form SS-8 (Determination of Employee's Work Status for Purposes of Federal Employment Taxes and Income Tax Withholding) with the IRS. Unfortunately, you can guess what the IRS usually responds:* employee. *And when you send in the form you're alerting the IRS to your situation.*

TAKE EVERY DEDUCTION YOU'RE ENTITLED TO

Now that you know your business is a business in the eyes of the IRS, you can start reaping the tax benefits of being in business for yourself. Unfortunately, 72% of all taxpayers overpay their taxes. In some cases it's out of ignorance, but for many it's because of *fear*!

► AUDIT MYTHS AND OTHER TALES OF HORROR

Many law-abiding, upstanding citizens refuse to take all the tax-saving deductions they are perfectly entitled to. That's because they're petrified of being audited by the IRS. They've been led to believe that if they take certain deductions, like the home-office deduction, they're in effect begging the IRS to audit them. They worry that just claiming certain perfectly legitimate deductions will red flag their return, triggering an IRS audit.

IRS audits are one of the biggest fears in this country. People come to me literally shaking because they received a *notice* from the IRS. In fact, it's not unusual for a client to call me up almost in tears because he or she received a letter from the IRS. They ask, "What will I do?" I ask what the letter says, and they tell me, "I don't know. I haven't opened it yet."

One woman refused to open an IRS letter until she was in my presence. Then she made me open it. It turned out that she had filled her tax return out improperly and overstated her income. The IRS was informing her that she was getting an additional refund!

The first time I represented a client at an IRS audit, I was as scared as my client. I had no idea what to expect. But when it was over, my client ended up with a refund. Boy, was I relieved.

This is not to say you don't have to fear the IRS. There are many stories of ruthless and abusive IRS agents. And many of those stories are probably true. However, extreme tactics are usually saved for suspected criminals, tax evaders, and political enemies. I've been representing taxpayers for over twenty years, and I personally know of only two incidents where the IRS used excessive force or ruthless tactics. One case involved a suspected drug dealer who hadn't filed a tax return for ten years, and the other was probably politically motivated.

That's not to say that it's okay for the IRS to ever act

abusively. The point is that if you're an average taxpayer, it's unlikely you'll be treated abusively—especially now. In the last couple of years it seems workers at the IRS are often friendlier and more helpful than ever before. It's as if they're trying to change their image. Do you think it's possible that the threat of the current income tax being replaced by a national consumption tax or flat tax might have something to do with that? After all, the proposal of the consumption tax and flat tax has been motivated, in large part, by many people's belief that the IRS is too powerful and acts like the gestapo. The consumption tax would eliminate the IRS for the most part, while the flat tax would reduce its size substantially.

What most people don't realize is that the IRS wants you to be scared of being audited. They want you to think they're like the KGB. They want you to be too terrified to cheat on your tax return. That's why they go after celebrities and prominent taxpayers who are more likely to make a splash on the front page. Coincidentally, this often happens every year just around April 15.

And in a lot of these cases, they'll intentionally give these public figures a hard time so that you won't even think of trying to cheat the government (or at least not as much as you would have otherwise).

Keep in mind that your chances of being audited are slim. Over two hundred million (that's 200,000,000) tax returns are filed every year. The IRS can't possibly stay on top of every return, especially with the severe budget cuts in recent years. What's their solution? They concentrate on auditing taxpayers who potentially will yield the most tax revenues. In 1995 they went after more sole proprietors than ever before, and still, less than 4% of tax returns containing Schedule C were audited. And what's more, according to some tax experts, 80% of all audits results in a "no change," refund, or compromise.

So why shouldn't you take all the deductions you're entitled to? In fact, if you have reasonable grounds to believe you're entitled to a deduction, but you're not 100% certain, follow the general principle: *when in doubt, deduct.* After all, there's only a slight chance you'll be audited. And even if you were, the chances are, at worst, you'll end up with a compromise that will leave you in a better financial position than if you had not taken the deduction at all. What's more, if you follow the substantiation guidelines provided throughout this book, you'll have nothing to worry about even if you get audited.

I'm not recommending that you cheat on your tax return. I strongly recommend you pay your taxes as required by law. What you'd save by filing a falsified tax return is not worth the restlessness, loss of sleep, and worry you'll suffer over the next three or, in some cases, seven years. And besides, there's no reason to cheat. If you implement the tax-saving techniques presented in this book, you'll reduce your tax bite plenty—and legally.

So—pay your taxes, but take the deductions that are due you! If you don't, you're doing yourself, your family, and this country a terrible disservice. It is your *right* to take all the deductions allowed by law. It's an aberration of our legal system for the IRS to perpetrate fear in citizens of this country until they are afraid to do what is their right to do.

As Judge Learned Hand said, "nobody owes any public duty to pay more than the law demands: taxes are enforced exactions, not voluntary contributions. To demand more in the name of morals is mere cant."

> ## CHOOSING THE RIGHT TAX PROFESSIONAL TO GET THE MOST OUT OF THIS BOOK

This book contains thousands of dollars worth of tax-saving deductions. Most of the ideas presented can be implemented right away. To help you get the most tax-saving benefits from these strategies, and to ensure you properly apply these tax-saving methods to your particular situation, consult a tax professional.

Tax professionals come in all different types and styles. There are accountants, CPAs, enrolled agents, bookkeepers, lawyers, and other general business consultants. Some specialize in working with large corporations, others with small businesses, and still others with self-employed professionals.

Most take a conservative posture when dealing with your tax savings. They'll only give you tax-savings advice that they know would never present a challenge from the IRS. They'll steer you away from doing anything that might raise even the slightest eyebrow of a revenue agent. In most cases these advisers are protecting themselves. At least one person in every workshop comes up to me infuriated at their accountant for not mentioning these tax-saving methods. However, under the tax law, tax professionals can be penalized if they improperly advise their clients or prepare tax returns for clients using inappropriate deductions. They don't want to take the chance of the IRS coming after them.

But it's you who loses out by not taking full advantage of every deduction allowable by law. You have more to gain by taking an aggressive stance. Here is how to find a tax professional who can help you do this.

1. When choosing a tax professional, get recommendations from friends and business associates and interview as many professionals as you can until you find one that's right for you. It would be great if you could find a tax adviser who specializes in your industry.

2. Choose an adviser whose clients fit the size of your business. Tax-saving strategies are different for someone who makes a couple of hundred thousand dollars each year as opposed to a business whose net profit is under $50,000.

3. Pick a consultant whose philosophical approach to taxes—how conservative or aggressive he or she is—is in accordance with yours. However, keep in mind that you don't want to hire a "Yes" person. You want someone whom you can bounce ideas back and forth with in order to arrive at creative solutions.

There's a difference between tax avoidance and tax evasion—about five years and $10,000! Tax avoidance is perfectly legal. The courts have consistently held that there is nothing wrong with arranging your affairs so as to keep your taxes as low as possible. Tax evasion is a crime.

My recommendation is to pick an adviser who has your interest as his or her primary concern. Your adviser should be willing to go as close to the line between tax avoidance and tax evasion as you feel comfortable with. However, your adviser should be knowledgeable enough to keep close to that line without crossing over to the tax-evasion side. After all, you don't want to spend sleepless nights worrying about "getting caught."

The tools in this book can be maximized by showing the ones that you want to implement to your tax adviser. There are thousands of dollars worth of tax-saving ideas in this book. You don't have to pay your adviser hundreds of dollars to learn them. Instead, you can spend a little time reviewing how they can best be applied to your situation.

▶ GUILTY UNTIL PROVEN INNOCENT

One basic tenet of the American legal system is that one is presumed innocent until proven guilty. That means that if you are suspected of breaking the law, the government must show proof of your guilt. This doctrine, incorporated into the Bill of Rights by our country's forefathers, was considered essential to guarantee freedom to its citizens.

This basic tenet of innocence has been sanctified in every area of our legal system—except one: the tax law. Under the tax law, you are effectively presumed guilty until proven innocent. This book is not intended to be a political dissertation on the IRS, so I will not discuss the legitimacy of this deviation from our Bill of Rights. However, it is important for you to realize that if you get audited, that's what you're dealing with.

For every deduction you claim, you must be able to *substantiate* it. If you can't substantiate a deduction, you'll be presumed to be, in effect, lying, and the deduction will be disallowed. The IRS is not required to prove the deduction isn't valid. It's your burden to prove it is valid. It's the same with income. For every deposit indicated on your bank statement, you must prove it isn't income and subject to tax. For example, if you get a gift of $500 from your family on your birthday and you deposit it in your bank, you must offer proof, if asked, that the $500 was other than taxable earned income.

> ▶ **AUDIT-PROOFING YOUR TAX RETURN**

By being able to substantiate everything you claim on your tax return you have effectively become *audit-proof.* That is, even in the highly unlikely event that you do get audited, you will feel assured that your deductions will be allowed.

Every deduction presented in this book is accompanied by instructions showing you how to substantiate that deduction. Every time I alert you to what you need to do in order to fulfill the substantiation requirements of the IRS, please take it seriously—*very seriously.* If you follow my simple instructions you will be audit-proof.

In addition to the substantiation requirements for each deduction there are three basic allies your business should have.

One is your **checking account.** I strongly recommend keeping a separate checking account for your business. This will enable you to more easily keep track of business expenses and income, keeping your records separate so that if audited you can provide the IRS the information they ask for and nothing more. It also helps establish that you are in business if you're in danger of being classified a hobbyist or employee as discussed in Part Two. Finally, your check register is a good source for identifying the nature of expenditures and deposits.

The second tool you'll need is **receipts.** I know, it's difficult to remember to ask for and keep those little pieces of paper. It's much easier to crumple them up and throw them on the ground, or simply walk away before getting them. But when you do that it's like throwing away money. In fact, that's exactly what you're doing: for just about every expenditure you claim as a deduction you need a receipt as proof.

In general, you need receipts for every purchase you claim a deduction for. However, you don't need receipts for expenses for which receipts are not normally provided, such as tips and taxi fares. Also, receipts are not required for expenses of less than $75 incurred for business meals or entertainment, or for expenses incurred while on the road. However, even when you don't need a receipt, you will still have to maintain a log recording all those expenditures.

And by the way, cancelled checks, as well as most credit-card receipts and statements, are not substitutes for receipts. Receipts contain the following necessary information proving your deduction: merchant's name, date of purchase, cost, and the item purchased. Some receipts do not describe the item purchased, in which case I suggested writing it in.

The third tool is your **appointment book.** Aside from helping you remember where you need to be and when, your appointment book contains (or will contain if it doesn't already) vital information to help you substantiate many deductions.

First, it helps establish the fact that your business really is a business and not a hobby. It lists all the business-related appointments and places you went during the year. In addition, as will be discussed later, it contains all the information necessary to substantiate business miles, deductions for meals and entertainment, and all other deductible expenses for which you don't have receipts.

Your appointment book is an invaluable aide to your business. However, there is always the risk of losing it. Don't expect sympathy from the IRS. That's why it's recommended to carry not more than two months of your appointment calendar at a time. Keep the records for the rest of the year safely stored.

▶ RECORD RETENTION

In my workshops, I'm invariably asked, "How long do I have to keep these records?" Since Richard Nixon's demise through the Watergate scandal, many attorneys advise their clients not to keep any records that can ever, in any way, be used against them. However, for tax purposes you do need to keep your records. And when it comes to record retention I am very conservative.

The general rule is that since the IRS has three years to audit your tax return, you should keep your records at least three years from the due date or the date you filed, whichever is later. However, the statute of limitations for some states is six years, as is the IRS's if the IRS suspects you understated your gross income by 25% or more. On top of all that, if anything in a tax return or any records are needed to substantiate a claim on a future year's return, those related records need to be available in case of an audit of that future year's return. For example, let's say you sell a house this year and defer the gain by reinvesting the money from the sale in a new house. You will need to keep all the records pertaining to the new house and the old house until at least three years after you sell the new house.

Unfortunately, there are many situations for which documents must be kept for an open-ended period of time. Therefore it is advisable to keep records for at least six years and even then discard only those items you know for sure will not be needed. Some tax advisers recommend that business owners keep their records eleven years in order to cover the time frame necessary for assessments, collection, and refund claim.

IV

CONVERTING EVERYDAY LIVING EXPENSES INTO BUSINESS DEDUCTIONS

Your business is *potentially* the best way to shelter your money from taxes. The key to turning your business into a tax shelter is to **convert everyday living expenses into business deductions.**

▶ TAX SAVINGS FROM DEDUCTIONS

The tax savings resulting from converting these expenses into business deductions is equivalent to receiving a discount or rebate on everything you spend money on. In other words, by owning your own business you automatically receive an invisible discount card. As explained in Part One, your discount is equivalent to your tax bracket. So if you pay $100 for computer supplies for your business, and your tax bracket is 50%, your cost is only $50. You pay $100, but at tax time you effectively receive a rebate of $50. Another way of looking at it is that if your tax bracket is 50%, you pay for one and get one free. If your tax bracket is 33%, you pay for two and get one free. Not a bad deal!

However, this discount card will not do you any good unless you know how to use it and you *do use it.* The following sections of Part Four provide simple guidelines to follow to convert your everyday costs of living into business deductions. Also, you will learn how to easily **audit-proof** your tax return by being able to provide the IRS with all the necessary proof to substantiate each deduction.

Use this information and reap the tax benefits of being self-employed. Don't use this information and you will have the IRS as a partner in your business.

All Ordinary and Necessary Business Expenses Are Deductible

The authority for converting everyday living expenses into business deductions is found in the Internal Revenue Code 162: "There shall be allowed as a deduction all ordinary and necessary expenses paid or incurred during the taxable year in carrying on any trade or business." To put it simply, all ordinary and necessary business expenses are deductible.

The term **"ordinary and necessary"** is very vague. The IRS attempts to clarify it in a Revenue Ruling by stating that if the expense is "appropriate and helpful in carrying on the business, and is commonly and frequently incurred in that type of business," then it's deductible. This clearly demonstrates that vagueness clarified with vagueness remains vague.

From a practical perspective, I have never witnessed the IRS deny a deduction for a small business on the grounds that it was not ordinary or necessary. Use your common sense and good judgement, and don't be greedy.

All the topics discussed in the following sections of Part Four are typical, ordinary, and necessary business expenses. As long as you're not greedy and maintain the suggested proof your deduction will be allowed.

Everything You Do, Everywhere You Go, Everyone You Meet

The trick to converting many everyday living expenses into business deductions is always to consider how what you're doing, where you're going, and who you're meeting can benefit your business.

When you go somewhere or do something, will it help you:

▶ Enhance your product or service?
▶ Add a new profit center?
▶ Discover new marketing techniques?
▶ Find less expensive suppliers?
▶ Contact potential new clients?

When you get together with someone is he or she:

▶ A client?
▶ A potential client?
▶ A source of referrals?

▶ A potential source of referrals?

▶ A business associate or employee?

Quiz: In "The Space Provided" below, list everyone you know who does not fit in one of those categories.

THE SPACE PROVIDED

↘ ↙

☐

If, in addition to looking at everything and everyone as being related to your business, you also utilize the audit-proofing techniques presented in the following sections, you will reap the major tax benefits of being your own boss.

▶ **SECTION A: IF YOU'RE ENTITLED TO THE HOME-OFFICE DEDUCTION, TAKE IT!**

Here are some of the everyday living expenses that this section will show you how to convert into business deductions:

▶ Home mortgage interest

▶ Real estate taxes

▶ Cost of your house (depreciation)

▶ Rent

▶ Office remodeling
▶ Utilities
▶ Home repairs
▶ Home maintenance
▶ Home insurance
▶ Security systems

Each year, thanks to modern technology, more and more Americans work at home. By the end of 1996 over forty million Americans worked at home. And that number is expected to rise by the turn of the century to include half of America's work force. There are many benefits to working at home, including less time wasted commuting to and from work and more time with the family. Given all the claims linking many of our social problems to the deterioration of the family, you would think the government would encourage people to work at home. Unfortunately, the tax law creates a disincentive to working at home. Under the tax code, office space away from your home is treated more favorably than office space at home. The IRS does not question the validity of a deduction for the cost of an office away from home. However, if you work at home the space is deductible only if you pass certain criteria, such as the space being used exclusively for business and nothing else.

In fact, the IRS would like you to believe the home-office deduction is *dead!* And there are three popular myths, unfortunately spread by many tax advisers, that perpetuate that theory. But guess what—the home-office deduction is *alive and well!* All you have to do to reap its tax savings is operate your business in such a way that you satisfy the requirements.

Debunking the Three Myths

> MYTH #1: Claiming the home-office deduction raises a "red flag."

It's true, the home-office deduction *used* to be on the IRS's hit list. In January 1993 the U.S. Supreme Court, in the *Soliman* case, ruled in favor of the IRS, making it more difficult to satisfy the requirements for the home-office deduction. As a result of this ruling, the IRS targeted tax returns that claimed that deduction. However, since then, the home-office deduction has been removed from the IRS's Top Hits Chart.

> MYTH #2: The tax savings aren't worth the hassle.

A recent survey of professional tax preparers indicates the average tax savings resulting from the home-office deduction ranges between $1,500 and $2,500. That's $1,500 to $2,500 extra in your pocket! Whether or not that's worth it to you is your decision. Personally, I can think of a lot of things to do with that money.

> MYTH #3: It's no longer possible to satisfy all the requirements.

The U.S. Supreme Court's 1993 decision in the *Soliman* case is credited with the creation of this myth. In that case, the IRS denied the home-office deduction to Dr. Soliman and the court ruled in favor of the IRS. This decision did make it more difficult for certain taxpayers to satisfy one of the home-office deduction requirements. However, most business owners claiming the deduction were not affected. And many of those that were affected can still claim the deduction by simply making a few changes in the way they conduct business. And, as you will see in a few pages, as part of the Taxpayer Relief Act of 1997, Congress essentially overturned the infamous *Soliman* case.

Qualifying for the Home-Office Deduction

If you use a space in your home for business and meet the following three criteria, you qualify for the home-office deduction.

1. Use the space on a *regular basis* for business, and
2. Use the space *exclusively* for business, and
3. Satisfy *any* of the following:
   a. The space used for your trade or business is in a **structure separate from your dwelling unit**, such as a detached garage, barn, or studio.
   b. **You meet or deal** with clients, patients, customers, or prospects in the normal course of your trade or business in your home.
   c. Your home is the **principal place of business** for your trade or business.

1. Regularly used for business. The Internal Revenue Code does not define "regular" as used in this situation. However, it does not mean you have to spend all or even most of your working time at home. For most self-employed owners, working at home two to three hours a day for four to five days each week would be sufficent.

2. Exclusively used for business. Exclusively means exclusively. You can use the space only for business purposes, not for anything else. Technically that means you can balance your business's checkbook in your office but not your personal checkbook. It also means your children can't do their homework or play games on the computer in your office.

However, contrary to popular belief, the space used for your business does not need to be an entire room with a door. You can designate a portion of any room, or any other part of your home, to be used exclusively for business purposes.

> **NOTE:** If you have more than one business and you use the space for both businesses, each must qualify for the home-office deduction in and of itself or the deduction will be denied to both businesses. This limitation also applies when you have a job in addition to your business and you bring work home. Unless the exclusive use is for the convenience of your employer, you will need to perform the take-home work in a part of the house other than your business's office.

3a. Separate structure. If you use a space regularly and exclusively for business but you do not meet with clients there and it is not your principal place of business, you can still be entitled to the deduction if the space is in a separate structure not attached to your house. This would include a detached garage, studio, or barn.

3b. Meeting with clients, patients, customers, or prospects. This criterion is satisfied by regularly meeting or dealing with clients, patients, customers, or prospects in the normal course of your business. These meetings or dealings must be substantial and integral to conducting your business. However, that does not mean all your meetings must take place at your home—just enough for it to be considered "regular."

NOTE: The people you meet or deal with *must* be physically present. Telephone conversations or e-mail correspondence are not enough.

3c. Principal place of business. How do you determine whether your home-office is your "principal place of business"? The law says that you look at all the "facts and circumstances" to determine if it is or not. Well, that's too vague a standard to give any guidance. The decision by the Supreme Court in the *Soliman* case helps clarify what you need to do for your home to be considered the "principal place of business."

Dr. Soliman, an anesthesiologist, used a space in his home regularly and exclusively for business. Although he did not meet with his patients there, he did use his office at home to maintain billing records, read medical journals, and prepare presentations and treatments. However, he administered anesthesia and treated patients at various hospitals, not at home. The court held that Dr. Soliman's home was not his "principal place of business" because the activities performed there were less important to his medical practice than the treatment he provided at the hospitals.

This ruling primarily affected business owners whose

major income-producing activities took place away from their homes, such as plumbers and other construction workers. It did not affect most attorneys, accountants, and others whose primary income-producing work takes place at home. And it's important to remember that had Dr. Soliman met with some clients at his home on a regular basis, in the normal course of business, he would still have been entitled to the home-office deduction even though it was not the "principal place of business."

The ruling in the *Soliman* case was not a popular one, other than with the IRS. So Congress, in its infinite wisdom (and desire to hold on to its constituency), included in the Taxpayer Relief Act of 1997 a provision that effectively overturns the *Soliman* case. Starting in 1999, the "principal place of business" definition will also include space at home if:

1. The Taxpayer uses it to conduct administrative or management activities; and
2. The Taxpayer does not conduct substantial administrative or management activities at any other fixed location.

The Determining Factors Prior to 1999

In order to determine whether your home-office is considered your "principal place of business" it's necessary to consider the following two primary factors:

1. Look at the relative importance of the business activities performed at each location you do business.

Where do the activities that are most important to your business take place? Where do your income-generating tasks take place? And most important, where do you meet with clients or deliver your goods or services?

If, after considering all those factors, you are still unable to determine your principal place of business then

2. Analyze the time spent at each location where you do business. Usually, the place you spend more than 50% of your time at is your principal place of business. If you still can't determine the principal place of business, it's possible you don't have one, and your home will not qualify as your principal place of business.

EXAMPLES

Here are some examples to help you understand how all these rules might apply to your situation:

Situation #1. Let's say you're a self-employed plumber. You repair and install plumbing in your customers' homes. Generally, you spend forty hours each week in the field and ten hours each week at your home-office doing paperwork, working with blueprints and talking to your customers on the phone. You also employ a full-time secretary who works for you exclusively in your home-office. If you were the plumber, would you take a deduction for an office at home? If you did and the IRS audited you, they would probably disallow the deduction. That's because the place where the plumber did the work that earned him his money was not in his home.

Situation #2. Let's say you teach at a local college. You spend 25 hours in the classroom and 35 hours at your home-office doing work related to what you teach. Your work at home might be essential, but your most important work will be deemed to take place at school, and therefore you will not be entitled to a home-office deduction.

Situation #3. Let's say you're a writer who spends 35 hours each week writing at your home-office. And you spend, on the average, another 15 hours each week doing research and meeting with publishers and interviewees. Are you going to take a home-office deduction? You bet!

Situation #4. Let's say you sell costume jewelry at craft shows, to retail stores, and through the mail. You spend 25 hours each week at home processing orders, keeping books, and ordering supplies. You also spend 15 hours each week at craft shows and at retail stores. Each of the activities generates approximately the same amount of money. Would you take a home-office deduction if you were in this situation? Since there is no significant income difference as to where you earn your money, look at the time spent at each location. You spend the most time at home. Therefore, you are entitled to the home-office deduction.

Exceptions: Day Care and Inventory Storage

There are two exceptions to these rules. If you use your home as a day-care facility you will be entitled to the home-office deduction even if all or some of the space is not used exclusively for the day-care operations. The second exception applies to storage of inventory. If you store inventory at your home on a regular, continuing basis and your home is the only fixed location of your business, then the space used to store inventory is deductible. This applies whether you're a retailer or a wholesaler.

THE PITFALLS

▶ **WATCH OUT!** *One of the benefits of being a home-owner is that the gain on the sale of your home will probably be tax-free. However, in order for the gain to be excluded from taxable income, the home sold must be your* primary residence. *And here's the bad news—the portion of your house that qualifies for the home-office deduction is* not *your residence; it's your* office. *As such, it does not qualify for the tax exclusion. For instance, if 15% of your home qualifies for the home-office deduction, then 15% of the gain on the sale of your home will be included in your taxable income. That's a nasty ending to a great deduction. Here's how to get around it.*

For Home Sales Prior to May 7, 1997

If you sold your home prior to May 7, 1997, you were not required to pay tax on the gain as long as you rein-vested the proceeds in another home within two years of the sale. However, as mentioned above, the gain on the portion of the house attributed to your home-office was taxable.

The way to get around this pitfall was—in the year of the sale—to make sure your office disqualified for the home-office deduction. The law stated that as long as you were *not* able to claim the home-office deduction in the year of the sale, you avoided the trap. That meant, if as of the day before the sale, your home no longer qualified for the deduction, you were safe.

However, it was wise to play it safe and allow several months of lag time between the date of disqualification for the home-office deduction and the date of sale, or cease using your home for your business by December 31 of the year preceding the year of sale.

If you did not reinvest the proceeds, there was another way for the gain to be tax-free. Taxpayers who were at least fifty-five years old at the time of the sale of their primary residence were entitled to exclude the first $125,000 of gain from the sale. This was a once-in-a-lifetime exclusion. Once you used the exclusion, even if it was for less than the full $125,000, that was it; you didn't get to do it again. As in the first pitfall, if a portion of the home sold was used as a home-office, then that portion would not qualify for the exclusion. However, if the part used for business did not qualify for the home-office deduction for at least two out of the last five years, then you didn't lose any part of the exclusion.

For Home-Sales after May 6, 1997

Under the new rules, every individual of *any* age who sells his or her home that was used as a principal residence and owned for at least two of the five years prior to the sale can exclude the gain from his or her taxable income. This exclusion, known as the Universal Exclusion, is limited to $250,000 for taxpayers who file as single, and $500,000 for those filing joint tax returns.

This is *not* a once-in-a-lifetime exclusion. It can be used over and over again, but only once every two years. That means, if on June 30, 1998, you sell you house for a gain of $250,000, the entire gain will be tax-free. Then, if you sell your next home on January 1, 2001, for a gain of $250,000, that gain will also be tax-free. And if there's a forced sale within the two-year required period, you'll be entitled to a partial exclusion. A "forced sale" includes having to change locations due to a change of employment, health, or certain other unforeseen circumstances.

Unfortunately, this exclusion applies only to your primary residence, if used as such, for at least two of the five years prior to the sale. And, as under the prior rules, the portion of your home qualifying for the home-office deduction is not considered part of your primary residence during the term it's used as an office.

As under the prior rules, the way to get around this is to make sure your office does not qualify for the home-office deduction for at least two of the five years prior to sale.

Another change under the new rules is that depreciation must be recaptured. That means even if you qualify for the Universal Exclusion, the gain on the sale of your home will still be taxed up to the depreciation deduction you were allowed while your home qualified for the home-office deduction. And that portion of the gain will be taxed as ordinary income, but with a cap of 25%.

Transition Rules

Even if you sell your house after May 6, 1997, you can still elect to apply the deferral or exclusion rules under the prior law if any of the following applies:

1. The sale of your home occurred between May 6, 1997, and August 5, 1997; or

2. The sale was made after August 5, 1997, under a binding contract in effect on August 5, 1997; or

3. Under prior law, the gain would not have been recognized because the replacement home was purchased on or before August 5, 1997. That is, if you sell your home after August 5, 1997, you can still elect to apply the rules as they existed under the prior law *if:* the replacement home was purchased prior to August 5, 1997, and the sale of the other home takes place within two years after the purchase date of the replacement home.

Disqualifying Your Home-Office Deduction

How do you disqualify your home-office deduction? It's easy. Remember, in order for the space to qualify for the home-office deduction, it must be used exclusively for business. That is, you can't do anything in there during the year that is not related to your business. Therefore, at any time during the year, take pictures that show the room was being used for an activity that disqualifies it as a home-office. For instance, put the TV in your office and throw a Super Bowl

> ▶ **TAX TIP:** *What if you sell your house at a loss? If part of the house qualified for the home-office deduction, be sure to maintain that status until the date of sale. That's because the portion of the loss attributed to your office will be deductible.*

party, or let the kids play on the computer. Don't forget to take lots of pictures. And, whatever you do, make it fun. After all, you're saving money.

Tax-Planning Strategies

Under the new rules, it is more complicated for home-owners to decide whether it is to their advantage to qualify for the home-office deduction. This is because if you claim the home-office deduction, a portion of the gain that would otherwise have been tax-free might be included in your taxable income. For example, if you sell your home and realize a $50,000 gain, under the new rules the gain will be tax-free. However, if 20% of your home qualified for the home-office deduction, then $10,000 (20% of the $50,000 gain) will be included in taxable income.

Before deciding whether to qualify a space in your home for the home-office deduction or not, compare the long-term tax savings you will derive from the home-office deduction versus the additional taxes that will result when you sell your home. In most cases, the benefits of the home-office deduction will significantly outweigh the additional tax.

Also, if you decide to designate a portion of your home to qualify for the home-office deduction, you will also need to determine whether to disqualify it for the deduction two years prior to selling your home. Remember, if your home does not qualify for the home-office deduction for at least two of the five years prior to sale, the Universal Exclusion will apply to the entire gain (other than the depreciation being recaptured).

Typical Situations

▶ If you rent rather than own your home, then take the home-office deduction.

▶ If you expect to sell your home at a loss, then continue to take the home-office deduction.

▶ If you're not planning to move for a long time, then it's probably to your advantage to take the home-office deduction at least up to two years prior to the sale of your home.

▶ If the gain expected to be realized on the sale of a home is not a lot, then most taxpayers will probably be better off qualifying for the home-office deduction up until the date of sale.

▶ If the value of your house has a high appreciation, then you will probably want to disqualify your house from the home-office deduction within at least two years from the time you expect to sell.

Determining the Portion of Your House Used for Business

To calculate your home-office deduction it's necessary to determine the percent of your home that is used for business. You can use any reasonable method that accurately reflects the portion of your home used for business.

The "square footage" method is the most commonly used. In this method, the percent of your home used for business is determined by dividing the square footage used for your business by the total square feet of your house.

Another commonly used method is the "rooms method." If all the rooms in your house are similar in size, you can just divide the number of rooms used for your business by the total number of rooms in the house. Use the method that gives the best result.

The Deductible Portion of House-Related Expenses

Generally, the portion of the expenses related to your home that are deductible is determined by the percentage determined in the above section. However, any expenses that are directly attributable to the portion of your home used for business will be allocated 100% to your business. For example, if you paint the office and no other part of the house, the cost of the painting will be 100% deductible. On the other hand, expenses incurred for the home that are totally unrelated to the office will not be deductible at all.

AUDIT-PROOFING TECHNIQUES

- ▶ **Take pictures.** At the beginning of each year, take lots of pictures that will help you prove the location in the house and the size of the room. Take pictures of business equipment and desks in the room, and make sure that nothing of a personal nature (like a bed) was in the room. You can even throw in a newspaper to help prove the date the pictures were taken.
- ▶ **Keep a record** of your times in and out of the office.
- ▶ **Keep logs showing** what you did in the office, when, and why.
- ▶ **Keep records of** the nature of the work you perform at home and elsewhere so you can substantiate that the most important tasks related to your work took place at home. This is important if you work out of your home but also perform services elsewhere.

- ► **Keep closing statements** from when you purchase or sell your house.
- ► **Keep receipts** for all major improvements made on your home.

EXAMPLE

As it turns out, Uncle Sammy did quit his job at Blockhead. He opened his own tax-preparation service, operating out of the basement in his home. At his office-at-home, he performs all his tax-preparation-related work, as well as meeting with most of his clients. The house is two thousand square feet and the portion he uses for an office is four hundred square feet. He rents the house for $1500 each month, which comes to $18,000 for the year. Other house-related expenses are utilities, $1800; repairs, cleaning, and maintenance, $1000; and insurance, $1100. As mentioned in Part One, his tax rates are federal, 28%; Colorado, 5%; and self-employment, 13%. (See tables on pages 65 and 67.)

> ► **SECTION B: DEDUCT *ALL* EQUIPMENT USED IN YOUR BUSINESS**

At any time, do you use any of the following equipment or furniture in your business? If yes, then you can deduct that item to the extent that it is used in your business. And this deduction applies to equipment and furniture in your home used for business purposes, even if your home does not qualify for the home-office deduction.

SAMMY'S TAX SAVINGS

1. Portion of Home Used for Business   .20

2. Expenses Allowed as Itemized Deduction or Business Deduction:

    a. Home Mortgage Interest $ N/A

    b. Real Estate Taxes $ N/A

    c. Total $ N/A

3. Line 1 × Line 2c $ N/A

4. Tax Saving #1 [Line 3 × .13 (Self-Employment Tax)] $ N/A

5. Other Home Deductions:

    a. Rent or Depreciation $18,000

    b. Utilities $ 1,800

    c. House Insurance $ 1,100

    d. Repairs and Maintenance $ 1,000

    e. Miscellaneous $

    f. Total Other Home Deductions $ 21,900

6. Line 1 × Line 5f $ 4,380

7. Tax Rate:

    a. Federal Income-Tax Rate   .28

    b. State and Local Income-Tax Rate   .5

    c. Self-Employment Tax Rate (Adjust if not all earnings are subject to self-employment tax as explained in Part One.)   .13

    d. Total Tax Rate   .46

8. Tax Savings #2 (Line 6 × Line 7d) $ 2,015

9. SAM'S TAX SAVINGS (Line 4 + Line 8) $ 2,015

TAX-SAVING STEPS YOU CAN DO TODAY: CREATING A HOME-OFFICE DEDUCTION

- Set aside a portion of your house for your business use. It could be a room or even just a part of a room.

- Remove all personal, non-business-related belongings.

- Take pictures of the room. To help prove the date, you can include a picture of a newspaper with that day's headlines. However, unless you are a sports reporter, don't show the sports section.

- Use that space exclusively for business.

- Meet there with patients, clients, or customers on a regular basis. Or make sure it otherwise qualifies as your principal place of business.

- Keep a brief log of how much time you worked at home and at other regular business locations (if you have any), and record what you did there.

▶ Computer
▶ Printer
▶ Computer-related equipment
▶ Fax machine
▶ Telephone
▶ Cellular phone
▶ Television
▶ VCR
▶ Stereo
▶ Camera
▶ Dining table
▶ Refrigerator
▶ Desks

CALCULATE YOUR TAX SAVINGS

1. Portion of Home Used for Business _____ .

2. Expenses Allowed as Itemized Deduction or Business Deduction:

    a. Home Mortgage Interest $ _____

    b. Real Estate Taxes $ _____

    c. Total $ _____

3. Line 1 × Line 2c. $ _____

4. Tax Saving #1 [Line 3 × .13 (Self-Employment Tax)] $ _____

5. Other Home Deductions:

    a. Rent or Depreciation   _____

    b. Utilities $ _____

    c. House Insurance $ _____

    d. Repairs and Maintenance $ _____

    e. Miscellaneous $ _____

    f. Total Other Home Deductions $ _____

6. Line 1 × Line 5f. $ _____

7. Tax Rate:

    a. Federal Income-Tax Rate   . _____

    b. State and Local Income-Tax Rate   . _____

    c. Self-Employment Tax Rate (Adjust if not all earnings are subject to self-employment tax. See note on page 6)   . _____

    d. Total Tax Rate   . _____

8. Tax Savings #2 (Line 6 × Line 7d) $ _____

9. YOUR TAX SAVINGS (Line 4 + Line 8) $ _____

▶ Bookcases
▶ Lamps
▶ Rugs
▶ Golf clubs
▶ Tennis equipment
▶ Skis

We didn't forget! Your *automobile* is equipment used in your business and technically belongs in this section. However, since it's such a major tax savings and since it has its own special rules, we devoted the entire next section to it.

Popular Misconceptions

One of the most commonly overlooked deductions I encounter every tax season is for equipment and furniture used in business. There are two popular misconceptions that create this oversight.

▼
MYTH #1: If you don't qualify for the home-office deduction you can't deduct equipment and furniture in your house that's used for your business.

Refer to the list of expenses in the beginning of the previous section (on the home-office deduction). Do you see listed any business equipment or furniture? No! Equipment and furniture used for your business is deductible to the extent that it's used for your business. And this is true for all assets, whether it's used away from your home or in your home. Whether or not your business qualifies for the home-office deduction has no effect.

▼

MYTH #2:   Only equipment and furniture used
           exclusively for business purposes are
           entitled to be claimed as business
           deductions.

The "exclusive" rule applies only to the home-office deduction. *All* equipment and furniture used in your business is deductible to the extent that it is used for business.

EXAMPLE

Let's say Uncle Sammy had a bed in the office for visiting relatives. Therefore, Uncle Sammy would not be entitled to the home-office deduction because the space was not used exclusively for business. In the room he kept a computer used in his business. His son, Fred, also used it to do homework. In fact, Fred used it 20% of the time, while the rest of the time the computer was used for the business. Can Sammy deduct the computer? Yes. Does he get a 100% deduction? No, the deduction is limited to 80%.

► **TIP:** *Again, all tangible personal assets used in your business are deductible. Look at the list above. Do you see anything strange? Golf clubs? Tennis equipment? Skis? These must only be for professional athletes, right? Wrong. As will be discussed in Part Four, Section D, you can deduct business entertainment. Equipment used while on business is deductible. For instance, if 50% of your golf outings qualify for the business-entertainment deduction, then you will be able to deduct half the cost of your golf clubs.*

Computing the Deduction

The general rule is that equipment and furniture must be depreciated. That is, you deduct their cost over the life of each asset. Our helpful friends at the IRS have been kind enough to supply us with the Useful Life Table. Unfortunately, you might not like what you see. For example, a computer's useful life is five years. Most businesses need to replace their computers after three years at the most.

Depreciation methods. There are two general ways you can depreciate your capital-asset purchases. One is called the *"straight-line method."* Using the method, you compute your depreciation for each year merely by dividing the cost by the asset's useful life. The result is that the depreciation is spread out evenly over the life of the asset. The other method is known as the *"accelerated method."* More often than not, business owners elect to accelerate the depreciation because it gives them a greater deduction in the earlier years. Although the overall deduction through the years is the same, most people would rather have a "bird in the hand than two in the bush."

In most situations, if you claim a deduction for depreciation, you will be able to choose the method that works best for you. However, for purchased assets that are classed as *listed property* (see below for definition), you can choose the accelerated method **only** if the property is used more than 50% for business purposes. If not, you must depreciate the asset using the straight-line method.

Write off 100% in the year of purchase. This may seem hard to believe, but the tax law actually contains a few breaks specifically designed for small businesses. One such tax break is the *Section 179 deduction.* Under this provision businesses may elect to write off the entire cost of equipment and furniture. However, there are certain limitations and criteria that must be satisfied in the year of purchase.

Criterion #1. The personal assets must be tangible—for example equipment and furniture. It does not include real property, improvements to real property, air conditioners, or heating units.

Criterion #2. The asset must be used in business in the year of purchase. For example, let's say you start a business in December 1997. You purchase equipment for your business in 1997 but you don't actually start using it till 1998. Because you did not start using it in your business in the year of purchase, you will not be able to claim a Section 179 deduction. However, starting in the year it's put to use, you will be able to write off its depreciation.

> ► **TIP:** *Don't forget! You can still depreciate equipment used in your business even if it was originally used only for non-business purposes. However, you will not be able to claim a Section 179 deduction. Many new business owners don't realize they can depreciate equipment and furniture previously used for non-business purposes that are now being used in their business.*

Criterion #3. The Section 179 deduction must be *elected* in the year of purchase. The way you elect it is by taking the deduction on Form 4562 at the time you file your original return for that year. If you don't make the election at that time, you cannot later elect it on an amended tax return unless the amended return is filed before the due date of the original return.

Criterion #4. The asset must be used more than 50% for business.

> ▶ **TIP:** *To get the maximum tax-saving benefits from listed property, be sure to use it more than 50% for your business. And continue doing so for its depreciable life.*

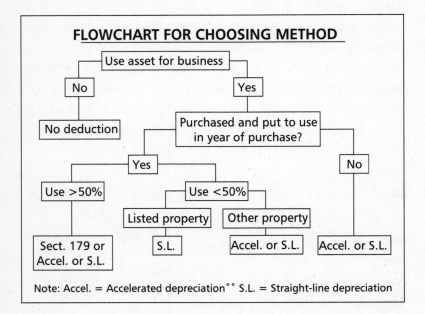

FLOWCHART FOR CHOOSING METHOD

Note: Accel. = Accelerated depreciation°° S.L. = Straight-line depreciation

The Section 179 deduction also has several limitations.

Limitation #1. The deduction is limited by the portion of time the asset is used for business purposes. For example, let's say you purchase a computer for $1,000 and use it 80%

of the time for business purposes. You may elect to deduct $800 (80% of $1,000) in the year of purchase.

Limitation #2. The following chart shows the maximum Section 179 deduction allowed each year. If your equipment and furniture purchases are greater than the allotted amount, the difference is depreciated. For example, in 1998 you purchase several items of equipment for your business, totaling $22,500. You would be allowed to claim the maximum Section 179 deduction of $18,500. The remaining $4,000 must be depreciated.

Year	Section 179 Limitation	Year	Section 179 Limitation
1997	$18,000	2001	$24,000
1998	$18,500	2002	$24,000
1999	$19,000	2003	$25,000
2000	$19,000		

Limitation #3. Your Section 179 deduction is limited to your adjusted taxable income. That is, in any given year you cannot use the amount of the Section 179 deduction that exceeds your adjusted taxable income. However, you can elect to carry over the unused portion of the Section 179 deduction to future years.

Limitation #4. The allowed Section 179 deduction is reduced if the total Section 179 property that was purchased during the year exceeds $200,000. The reduction is dollar for dollar. For example, in 1998 the Section 179 limitation is $18,500 (see chart, page 73). If in that year you purchase $190,000 of equipment, you will be able to claim a Section 179 deduction for $18,500 and depreciate the difference of $171,500. If your total equipment purchases for that year were $210,000, then your allowed Section 179 deduction would be $8,500 (18,500 less $10,000). And lastly, if your equipment purchases were $218,500 or more, you would not be able to claim any Section 179 deduction for that year.

The Tax-Saving Benefit

Using equipment in your business that you would have purchased anyway for personal purposes effectively reduces its cost to you. Here's an example. Before Uncle Sammy began his business, he decided his family needed a computer and printer. He needed them for writing letters to family and friends; Iris needed them for the household bud-

SAMMY'S TAX SAVINGS		
	Personal Use 100%	Business Use 75%
1. Price of Computer and Printer	$ 3,500	$ 3,500
2. Business Use	0%	75%
3. Deductible Portion (Line 1 × Line 2)	0	$ 2,625
4. Tax Bracket	46%	46%
5. Tax Savings (Line 3 × Line 4)	0	$ 1,207
6. After-Tax Cost (Line 1 less Line 5)	$ 3,500	$ 2,293

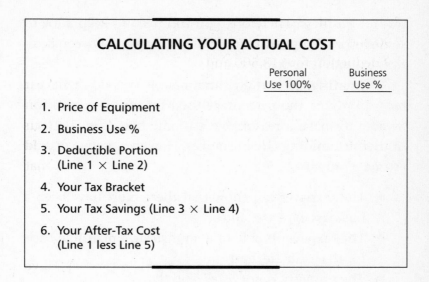

	Personal Use 100%	Business Use %
CALCULATING YOUR ACTUAL COST		
1. Price of Equipment		
2. Business Use %		
3. Deductible Portion (Line 1 × Line 2)		
4. Your Tax Bracket		
5. Your Tax Savings (Line 3 × Line 4)		
6. Your After-Tax Cost (Line 1 less Line 5)		

get and record keeping; and the children needed them for homework and computer games. Unfortunately, the purchase price of $3,500 was over his budget. However, once he decided to go into business for himself, the cost of the computer and printer became a business deduction. Sammy used the computer and printer for business 75% of the time. The purchase price was still $3,500; however, because of the tax savings, he was able to get this equipment for the equivalent of a 46% discount. In other words, after the tax savings the cost was $2293, a $1207 savings.

AUDIT-PROOFING TECHNIQUES

Receipts. When you purchase equipment or furniture, make sure you get a receipt. And hold on to that receipt until at least three years after you sell the asset.

Record of business use. The general rule is that you must be able to prove the percentage of use of the asset that was for business. Therefore, you will need to keep a log or some record that substantiates the allocation between business use and non-business use.

Estimating. In certain situations, if you don't have a record proving the percentage used for business, you will be able to make a reasonable estimate based on the facts of the surrounding circumstances. However, taxpayers can estimate only if:

▶ The taxpayer can show that there must have been a business expense, and

▶ The taxpayer is able to demonstrate a plausible basis for the estimate, and

▶ The property is not *listed property.*

Listed Property. In an attempt to limit the deduction for assets commonly used for both business and personal purposes the IRS created a new category of assets called *Listed Property.*

Listed property includes:

▶ Computers

▶ Computer-related equipment including fax machines and printers

▶ Any property generally used for communication, entertainment, recreation, or amusement purposes, such as cellular phones, TV, VCR, or cameras

▶ Any passenger automobile

▶ Any other property used as a means of transportation

Adequate records. For all listed-property assets you are required to keep adequate records, such as a written daily log, that shows the amount, date, and business purpose of each business use. Also you need to establish total annual use.

You must also record the business purpose of each use unless it can be determined by the surrounding facts and circumstances, such as a salesperson visiting customers on an established sales route.

However, any asset used solely for business purposes and kept at a regular business establishment is not subject to the record-keeping requirements for listed property. "A regular business establishment" includes a portion of your home used regularly and exclusively for business, even if it doesn't qualify for the home-office deduction.

NOTE: If you have two businesses, it will be necessary to keep track of the asset's use in each business.

The Shortcut Record-Keeping Method

If you're like most taxpayers, you'd rather not waste your time with record keeping. And the people who don't mind record keeping usually don't have the time to do it anyway. For all those who can think of something better to do than spend their time logging in and out every time they use a piece of equipment, there *is* a shortcut. Instead of logging your use of the equipment for the entire year, you can keep them for just a portion, if that part of the year is representative of the entire year. Here are a couple of periods that have been allowed:

▶ 90 consecutive days
▶ first week of every month

> ▶ SECTION C: GETTING THE MOST "TSPM" OUT OF
> YOUR CAR

Most people are concerned about their car's MPG (miles per gallon). The higher the miles per gallon, the lower the cost of operating their car. Another way to reduce the cost of operating your car is to make sure you get the highest **TSPM** out of your car. TSPM? That's **tax savings per mile!**

Expenses covered:

- ▶ Cost of vehicle
- ▶ Gas
- ▶ Oil change
- ▶ Auto supplies
- ▶ Tires
- ▶ Auto repairs and maintenance
- ▶ Car wash
- ▶ Auto-lease payments
- ▶ License fee
- ▶ Registration fee
- ▶ Parking
- ▶ Tolls
- ▶ Auto interest
- ▶ Auto-repair tools

In the previous section we discussed, in part, equipment used for both business and personal purposes. However, we didn't include the piece of equipment that's most commonly used for these dual purposes: the automobile. Not only is it the piece of equipment most often used for both purposes, it's also the deduction that's most commonly under-utilized. Sometimes taxpayers claim less of a deduction than they're entitled to because they just don't know business miles are deductible; other times, they don't realize how much of a tax savings they can get, even if they use the standard 31 cents per mile; but mostly they're under the misconception that the hassles of fulfilling the record-keeping requirements aren't worth it at any cost.

What's Deductible, What's Not

Use of your car for business purposes is deductible. Use of your car for personal use is not deductible. Simple? Not quite.

Commuting. Under the Internal Revenue Code you can claim a business deduction for any and all ordinary and necessary expenses incurred in a trade or business for the production of income. So shouldn't the cost of going between your home and work be deductible? Isn't it necessary for you to make the trip to earn money? Sure it is. For many people, commuting is not only very time-consuming but also puts a lot of miles on your vehicle. But the IRS has made a unique transportation category called "commuting expenses" and has declared that those expenses are not deductible.

Commuting expenses include all transportation expenses (such as mileage, tolls, bus, and taxi) between your residence and your main or *regular* place of business.

Doing Business on the way to work. Some of you might be thinking, "I know how to get around this. I'll use commuting time to make business calls on my cellular phone." Or, "I can drive with my partner to work and discuss business." You are not the first to come up with those ideas. Unfortunately, working during a trip to or from the office does not change the drive from non-deductible commuting miles to a business deduction.

Here's What You Can Deduct

Office at home. Another benefit of conducting your business out of your home is that *all* transportation expenses to and from your home, for any business-related purpose, are deductible.

Put on your thinking caps. What if your home is a regular place of business but it doesn't qualify for a home-office deduction?

Are transportation expenses between your home and another place of business deductible? For example, remember our plumber friend in the last chapter? He doesn't qualify for the home-office deduction, but can he write off the cost of driving to his clients?

Here's a surprise. In *Walker v. Commissioner,* a 1993 case, the Tax Court ruled that even though the taxpayer did not qualify for the home-office deduction, he was still entitled to deduct his transportation costs around town.

Not surprisingly, the IRS does not agree with this decision, and it has announced that it will continue to challenge these deductions made by the taxpayers.

If you were the plumber, would you take the deduction? The courts are a higher authority than the IRS. If you follow the court's ruling, you will not be making a frivolous claim.

You have a very valid reason to believe the deduction is proper.

The Walker case does not apply if your regular place of business is outside your home, in which case trips between your office-at-home that is not your principle place of business and outside locations are not deductible.

Also, don't forget the home-office rules change going into effect in 1999. Most business owners, like plumbers, for example, doing their administrative or management activities at home will qualify for the home-office deduction. Then, the I.R.S. will have no cause to challenge the mileage deduction.

Office away from home. If your office is away from your home, then the cost of getting from your home to the office will be deemed commuting and will not be deductible. However, if you have a regular place of business, then all transportation costs from your home to *temporary* work locations are deductible. This means that if you have a regular business location, whether at home or elsewhere, and you go directly from you home to a customer, those transportation expenses will be deductible. So if on the way to your office you stop at a client, and on the way home you stop to see another client, all your travels for the day will be deductible.

▶ **WATCH OUT!** *If you stop at a particular client too often, the IRS will consider the site to be one of your regular places of business and will not allow the deduction.*

It is possible that you don't have a *regular* place of business. In that case, none of your transportation costs, even to temporary work sites, will be deductible. However, if the temporary location is outside the metropolitan area you ordinarily work in, transportation costs to that location will be deductible.

The following chart will help you determine the deductibility of local transportation expenses in situations where your office is away from home.

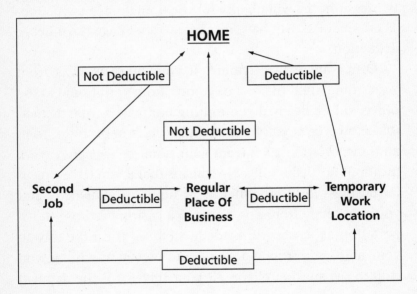

Calculating the Deduction: Standard Versus Actual—Which Do I Choose?

In the year you start using your vehicle in your business, you can choose between the *standard deduction* and the *actual deduction*. How do you decide? It's simple: choose the one which gives you the greatest deduction.

The Standard Deduction. If you like simplicity, it doesn't get any simpler than this. To compute your automobile deduction under the standard method, multiply your business miles by that year's rate. In 1997 the rate was 31.5 cents per mile. Since you're getting a set deduction per mile, you do not need to have receipts or maintain records of your vehicle-related expenditures. However, as will be discussed shortly, you do need to record your business miles and total miles for the year.

Not everyone is permitted to choose the standard deduction. You cannot use this method if you:

- ▶ Do not own the vehicle; for example, use leased or borrowed vehicles
- ▶ Use the vehicle for hire, such as a taxi
- ▶ Operate two or more vehicles simultaneously for the same business (you can use them alternately, just not have two drivers use the cars at the same time.)
- ▶ Claimed accelerated depreciation or a Section 179 deduction in the previous year for that vehicle

The Actual Method. If you don't qualify for the standard mileage deduction or if the cost of operating your vehicle is greater than the allowed standard rate, you can compute your automobile deduction using the actual method. Under this method you include all the costs of operating your car and multiply the total by the percentage you used your car for business.

The percentage is derived simply. Divide your business miles by the total miles driven during the year. If you drove your car 5,000 business miles and 10,000 total miles, then your business use is 50%. The costs that qualify as part of

CHOOSING-THE-METHOD CHART

1. Total Miles Driven _____

2. Business Miles _____

3. Business Percentage _____
   (Line 2 Divided by Line 1)

4. Car Costs:

   Gas $ _____

   Repairs and Maintenance $ _____

   Insurance $ _____

   Registration Fee $ _____

   Depreciation $ _____

   Other* $ _____

5. Total Car Costs $ _____

6. Automobile Deduction:

   Actual Method (Line 5 × Line 3) $ _____

   Standard Method $ _____

      [Line 2 × .315 (rate for 1997)]

*Do not include interest, parking, or tolls, since they're
deductible under either method.

the automobile deduction include depreciation, the Section
179 deduction, lease payments, gas, oil, repairs, maintenance, car washes, tires, license, and insurance.

Extra Deductions. Even if you elect the standard-
mileage approach, you can also deduct the business portion
of interest on a car loan and the state and local personal-
property-tax portion of your auto-registration fee. In add-

tion, all your business-related parking fees and tolls are deductible. However, you cannot deduct the amount of those that are related to your cost of commuting.

Do you do your own repairs and maintenance on your vehicle? If so, the equipment and supplies you use to do the work are deductible to the extent that you use your car for business.

Buy a Sport-Recreation Vehicle and Save Money. As discussed in the prior section, equipment used in business is depreciated over its useful life. You may elect to deduct its cost in the year of purchase under Section 179. However, the deduction under Section 179 cannot exceed a certain amount each year ($18,000 for 1997, and $18,500 for 1998). Unfortunately, the limitations are even stricter for cars. The combined depreciation and Section 179 deductions for 1997 for cars could not exceed $3,160 in the year of purchase. In the second year, the deduction was limited to $5,000. In the third year, the limitation was $3,050; and each year thereafter, until the car is written off, the limit is only $1,775. Therefore, if you purchase a $40,000 vehicle in 1997 and use it 100% for business, it will not be fully written off until the year 2016. Because of this limitation, it may pay to lease your vehicle rather than buy.

However, this limitation does not apply to:

▶ An ambulance or hearse used directly in a business
▶ A vehicle for hire, or
▶ *A vehicle with an unloaded gross weight of more than 6,000 pounds*

You might be surprised how many vehicles weight 6,015 pounds. Car manufacturers know that the ability to write a

vehicle off faster is a great selling point. Partly for this reason, many sport-recreation vehicles fit within this category,
such as Suburbans, Land Rovers, and Toyota Land Cruisers.
Many pickup trucks also qualify for this special treatment.

Look at the following chart. It shows why Uncle Sammy
decided on a $32,500 sport-recreation vehicle weighing
more then 6,000 pounds, instead of a $32,500 regular car
weighing less than 6,000 pounds. As you can see, the tax
savings is the same. However, with the heavier vehicle, the
vehicle is totally written off in the first six years, with most
of the tax savings in year one, whereas it takes 15 years for
the other vehicle to be totally written off.

Tax Year	Weight Less than 6,000 Pounds		Weight More than 6,000 Pounds	
	Depreciation + 179 Deduction	Tax Savings (Assumes 46% Tax Bracket)	Depreciation + 179 Deduction	Tax Savings (Assumes 46% Tax Bracket)
1997	$ 3,160	1,454	20,500	9,430
1998	5,000	2,300	4,800	2,208
1999	3,050	1,400	2,880	1,325
2000	1,775	816	1,728	795
2001	1,775	816	1,728	795
2002	1,775	816	864	397
2003–2010	1,775 (each year)	816 (each year)		
2011	1,765	820		
Total	$32,500	14,950	32,500	14,950

One plus one is greater than two.

	Yes	No
Do you own two cars?	☐	☐
Do you use just one of them for business purposes?	☐	☐
Do you use the Actual Method for determining your automobile deduction?	☐	☐

If you answer "yes" to all three questions, then consider using both cars for your business.

A common misconception is that you save tax dollars by devoting one car to business and the other to personal purposes. In actuality, if you use the standard-mileage deduction method, it will not matter. However, if you use the actual method you will most likely save more on your taxes by splitting the use of each vehicle between personal and business purposes.

EXAMPLE

Uncle Sammy's situation illustrates this principle. Uncle Sammy and Aunt Iris own two cars, which they drive a total of 28,000 miles. Sammy's business miles are 20,000, and his personal miles are 8,000. By driving all 20,000 business miles on just one of the cars, his business deduction is $4,000, for a $1,840 tax reduction. Notice that the business percentage is 100%. However, by splitting the business mileage between the two cars the business percentage is now 130%. And the tax reduction is $2,047.

SAMMY'S MILEAGE DEDUCTIONS

	One Business Car			Two Business Cars		
	Car 1	Car 2	Total	Car 1	Car 2	Total
Total Miles	20,000	8,000	28,000	20,000	8,000	28,000
Business Miles	20,000	-0-	20,000	16,000	4,000	20,000
Business %	100%	-0-	100%	80%	50%	130%
Total Costs (includes deprec.)	$4,000	$2,500	$6,500	$4,000	$2,500	$6,500
Total Deduction	$4,000	-0-	$4,000	$3,200	$1,250	$4,450
Tax Bracket	—	—	46%			46%
Tax Savings			$1,840			$2,047

YOUR MILEAGE DEDUCTIONS

	One Business Car			Two Business Cars		
	Car 1	Car 2	Total	Car 1	Car 2	Total
Total Miles						
Business Miles						
Business %						
Total Costs (includes deprec.)						
Total Deduction						
Tax Bracket						
Tax Savings						

AUDIT-PROOFING TECHNIQUES

Here's a situation Uncle Sammy encounters in his tax-preparation business every tax season. A client comes in. During the course of the interview Sammy innocently asks, "Do you use your car for business?" The client says, "Yes." Sam asks him the number of miles he drive for business. The client looks up at the ceiling. Sam looks up too, knowing the IRS regulations require mileage to be recorded. If it isn't, then the mileage deduction will be denied. Sam figures the ceiling is as good a place as any to look. The client says, "10,000 miles." What's wrong with this picture?

Suppose you're an IRS auditor. You know mileage needs to be recorded in writing to be deductible. Would you be suspicious seeing that someone drove exactly 10,000 miles? I'll give you a hint. Mount McKinley happens to be exactly 29,000 feet high. However, they figured nobody would believe that, so it's recorded as 29,001 feet.

By the way, on every tax return claiming an automobile deduction, you are asked to check the "yes" box if you have substantiation in writing to support the deduction. Don't forget, you also sign the tax return. So if you answer falsely you've perjured yourself. Not a good idea!

I hope you're not thinking like my cousin Will-Do Tomoro. He filed his 1993 tax return claiming an automobile deduction. However, he didn't record the required mileage. He figured his chances of being audited were slim (which was true). And he thought that if he happened to get notified of an audit, he'd have plenty of time to put something together. Sure enough, fate responded to this irresistible temptation, and the IRS invited Will-Do to be their honored guest. Just as Will-Do guessed, he had plenty of time to put together a mileage log. He went to the office supply store and purchased an appointment book. Using different colored pens and pencils, he filled in the mileage information throughout the year. He creased the pages, spilled coffee on them, and played modern artist on the pages with pizza sauce. He created a masterpiece. Unfortunately, he overlooked just one thing. The year on the appointment book was 1995, not 1993. Every now and then I visit Will-Do. He will be getting out in time to file his tax return for the year 2000.

The moral: Keep a mileage log and promise you Will-Do it today and not put it off for Tomoro.

The EZ Mileage Log. There's really no excuse not to keep a mileage log. It's simple. Remember, many pages ago we discussed your ally the appointment book? Well, here's one of the ways it will come in handy. You should be already recording where you have to go, when you have to be there, and whom you're meeting there. Now, all you have to do is write in the business purpose next to your appointment, fill in the number of miles, and circle it. And you don't even have to do it every day. You can fill it in on a weekly basis. If on a particular day you make a series of uninterrupted business stops, then a total mileage figure for the day will be sufficient.

Still not simple enough? Then instead of keeping a record for the whole year, you're allowed to keep a record of a portion of the year that's representative of the entire year. For example, any 90 consecutive days, or the first week of every month. However, you will need to demonstrate that the period selected is representative of the rest of the year.

By the way, if you have commuting miles, you will also need to log those.

At the end of the year, add up all your circled numbers and voila! You have your total business miles for the year. For the total miles for the year, all you have to do is record your odometer reading on January 1st of each year.

Personally, I know I can't rely on my memory. At the time I purchase my appointment book for the coming year, I write on the January 1st page a reminder to record the odometer reading. But I also know I may never look at the New Year's Day page, especially after the New Year's Eve celebration, so I make another note on January 2nd.

Receipts. If you elect the standard mileage method you are not required to have receipts or substantiate in any other way your expenses related to your automobile deduction. However, you will still need the mileage log. If you elect the actual method, receipts are not required for any

---

TAX-SAVING STEPS YOU CAN TAKE TODAY:
START A MILEAGE LOG

* In your appointment book, under today's date, record your odometer reading. If you can determine the mileage as of a date closer to the beginning of the year, that would be better. **HINT:** Look at repair invoices. Most auto mechanics record odometer readings on your bill.

* Under today's date, list all the places you went for your business, and next to each record the mileage and circle it. (If necessary, also record the purpose.)

* Put all receipts for car-related expenses in a folder marked "car receipts."

purchase less than $75. However, if you don't have the receipt, you will need the information recorded on a log or in your appointment book. As recommended earlier, it's best to keep all receipts, even those for purchases less than $75.

To help keep track of all your automobile expenses, a credit card dedicated to paying only your automobile expenses comes in handy.

► **SECTION D: MEALS, ENTERTAINMENT, AND GIFTS**

Everyday living expenses that are covered in this section include:

- ► **Going out to eat**, including food, beverages, tax, tips, and mileage
- ► **Going out on the town**, such as theater or sporting events
- ► **Recreational activities**, including golf, bowling, or skiing
- ► **Recreational equipment**, such as golf clubs, bowling balls, or skis
- ► Entertaining at home
- ► Gifts

The Three Primary Principles

In this section you will learn how you can deduct meals, entertainment, and gifts. These are common everyday living expenses. Throughout this section, keep in mind the three primary principles of converting everyday living expenses into business deductions discussed earlier:

Principle #1: *All everyday living expenses can be converted into business deductions, if you know how.*

Principle #2: *Whatever you do, wherever you go, and whomever you meet can be related to your business.*

Principle #3: *You have the right to conduct your life and business in a way that enables you to utilize the tax benefits afforded self-employed business owners. "Nobody owes any public duty to pay more than the law demands."*

The "Three-Martini Lunch" Is Now the "Burger and Glass of Water Lunch"

It used to be when you went out for a meal during the workday with a business associate, such as a client, you were allowed to deduct 100% of the cost of the meal, including drinks. It became known as the "three-martini lunch."

It seemed everybody was going out on business lunches and writing them off. Fancy restaurants loved it. They were packed during what would otherwise be a low-traffic part of the day. Then the tax law was changed. The three-martini lunch became the 2.4-martini lunch. That's when the deduction for meals and entertainment became limited to 80% of its cost.

In and of itself, that wasn't too bad. However, what qualified for the deduction was also drastically restricted. No longer were businesses willing to pay for extravagant lunches. Martinis became Perrier, and filet mignon got ground up into hamburgers. Many fancy restaurants that once prospered closed their doors and became fast-food chains or pizza parlors.

And now, what was once the three-martini lunch has become the "I'll have a burger and a glass of water" lunch. That's because as of January 1, 1995, only 50% of the cost for business meals and entertainment is deductible.

Pay for Three, Get One Free

Don't get disheartened. Even though you do not get to deduct 100% of business meals and entertainment expenses, the deduction you get is still worth your while. Let's say your tax bracket is 50%. That means you still get a tax savings of 25% of your bill for meals and entertainment. For example, you go out to eat with a client and both your spouses. The bill comes to $100. You receive a deduction of $50, which gives you a tax savings of $25. In other words, the meal really costs you $75. Here's another way of looking at it: by being your own boss, you receive an automatic, invisible discount card. With this card, with every entertainment expense you get one free for every three you pay for. For every four meals, you pay for only three. For every four rounds of golf, you pay for only three. For every four lift-tickets you pay for three and get one free.

Know the Rules, Deduct the Cost

You can deduct the cost of *entertainment* that is:

▶ Ordinary and necessary; *and*
▶ With a client, customer or employee; *and*
▶ Related to your business

Entertainment. According to the IRS, "Entertainment includes any activity generally considered to provide entertainment, amusement, or recreation, and includes meals provided to a customer or client." Typical types of entertainment include meals at restaurants or at home; theater; movies; sporting events; and recreational activities such as golf and skiing.

Meals while on business trips can be deducted under the travel rules instead of under these entertainment rules. Part Four, Section E discusses how meals that are not deductible at home become deductible while on the road.

Ordinary and necessary. Per IRS Publication 463, "An ordinary expense is one that is common and accepted in your field of business, trade, or profession." And, "A necessary expense is one that is helpful and appropriate, although not necessarily indispensable, for your business." Expenses that might be extravagant for one person might be perfectly acceptable for another. It depends on the type of business and the other facts and circumstances. I wouldn't consider trying to write off flying to Paris for lunch. (Then again, I wouldn't consider going on such an extravaganza in the first place.) But the same trip might be perfectly acceptable for someone like Bill Gates, who's got business all over the world, and for whom the expense might be small change.

Client, customer, or employee. You cannot entertain just anyone to get the deduction. The entertainment deduction is limited to entertaining:

▶ Clients or customers
▶ Potential clients or customers
▶ Sources of referral
▶ Potential sources of referral
▶ Suppliers
▶ Employees

Did I say "limited"? Do you know anyone who doesn't fit in one of these categories? As mentioned earlier, *everyone* can be related to your business in some way or other. However, as with every rule, there is an exception. Closely connected family members, such as spouses, are generally excluded from eligible entertainees. However, as will soon be discussed, under certain circumstances the costs of their entertainment is also deductible.

Related to your business. In order to satisfy the *"related to your business"* criterion, the entertainment must fall into *one* of the following three categories:

1. The entertainment takes place in a **clear business setting;** or
2. The **main purpose** of the entertainment was the active conducting of business, and you engaged in business with the person during the entertainment period, and you had more than a general expectation of getting income or some other specific business benefit; or

3. The entertainment is associated with your trade or business and either immediately precedes or follows a **substantial business discussion**

What does this all mean, on a practical level, to you?

Deducting meals. If you want to deduct the cost of a meal, you will need to have a business discussion either during, immediately before, or immediately after the meal. As part of the discussion, you must show you had the purpose of getting income or some other specific business benefit.

Deducting other forms of entertainment. The IRS does not consider it possible to have a substantial business discussion during an entertainment activity other than a quiet meal. For example, a professional hockey game is not considered conducive to discussing business. They might have a point there. But what about during a round of golf? If you've ever played, you know it's quiet and there's lots of time to talk shop. However, the powers that be at the IRS probably play on different golf courses than the rest of us are accustomed to.

In general, for entertainment, other than quiet meals, the business discussion must take place either immediately before or immediately after the entertainment. For meals, the discussion can take place before, during, or after the meal.

What Is a *Substantial Business Discussion?*

A substantial business discussion is a discussion, meeting, negotiation, or other business transaction to get income or some other specific business benefit. *It does not have to be for any specified amount of time!* In other words, it's the quality of the discussion that counts, not the quantity. How long does it take you to make a pitch for your business?

Immediately Before, Immediately After

Situation #1. You take a client out to eat and discuss business during the meal. Deductible? Yes.

Situation #2. You treat a client to a football game. While driving there together, you have a substantial business discussion. Deductible? Yes, because the discussion took place immediately before the entertainment.

Situation #3 is the same as situation #2, except you meet the client at the game. That morning you had a substantial business discussion with that client over the phone. Is the cost of the game deductible? Yes. *Immediately before or after* includes discussions that take place any time during the day of the entertainment.

And in certain situations, expenses for entertainment are deductible even though the entertainment takes place the day before or after the business discussion. For example, say that clients came in from out of town the night before a meeting. You can deduct the cost of taking them out to eat that night, even though the business meeting didn't take place till the following day.

Whom Can You Pay for and Deduct?

The general rule is you can deduct the cost of entertainment for a person with whom you engaged in the business discussion. You can also deduct the cost for spouses and other "closely connected persons" if you can show a clear business purpose for their presence. For example, you may deduct for your client's spouse and your spouse joining you because it's impractical to entertain your client without his or her spouse.

How about taking your children, parents, or significant others along? Are they considered *closely connected?* It seems children would be included, but as of this writing the line of demarcation is unclear.

Let's say you take your client out to eat to discuss a business deal. Both your spouses join you, along with your client's best friend. Is it all deductible? No, unless the friend is a potential client or source of referrals and the two of you engage in a substantial business discussion.

How about the portion of the bill pertaining to yourself such as the cost of the meal you ate, or the cost of your ticket?

The general rule is that the portion of the entertainment expense that is for yourself is only deductible to the extent that it exceeds the amount you would normally spend on yourself. Uh-oh! However, the IRS does not usually enforce this rule, and they do not intend to. The only time they do enforce it is against taxpayers who overindulge. As long as you don't overindulge you can write off all of your share of entertainment that qualifies for a business deduction.

Dutch treat. How about if you pay for only your share of the tab: is that deductible? Yes, as long as the entertainment qualifies as a business deduction. However, stay on the safe side. Don't take too much advantage of the IRS's generosity. Limit your dutch-treat meals to no more than one hundred breakfasts, one hundred lunches, and one hundred dinners per year.

Protecting yourself. If you want to be sure the IRS doesn't challenge your share of the deduction, have proof that you spend more money with a client, employee, or prospect than you would by yourself. For example, show that when you go out for lunch alone you typically spend no more than $3, but when you go out on business you spend $15. Or, better yet, show that the *only* time you go out for meals, drinks, or whatever is when it's business-related.

Home Entertainment

I don't know about you, but I would rather eat at home. The food's better, and it's less crowded, not smoky, and less expensive. But is it deductible? You bet! If you invite a client or anyone else over, and you satisfy the entertainment rules, your costs will be deductible.

There's more to the entertainment deduction than most people think. Obviously, the cost of the qualifying entertainment itself is deductible: the cost of a meal, beverages, tips, and taxes; the cost of going to the theater or sporting event (limited to the face value of the ticket); the admission cost of a recreational activity like a green fee and ski-lift ticket.

But how about ancillary costs, such as transportation and equipment used in the activity. Equipment? Yes, such as the cost of ski equipment and golf equipment. These are deductible, as is all other equipment used in business. For example, if 80% of your golf outings are business related, then 80% of the cost of your golf equipment is eligible to be deducted as business equipment.

As to transportation to and from entertainment activities, some is deductible and some is not. If the business discussion takes place at the site of the entertainment, then the related transportation will be deductible. However, if the discussion takes place prior to or after the activity and at a different location, the cost of transportation is not deductible.

As we mentioned earlier, only 50% of the entertainment expense is deductible. However, related transportation and equipment expenses, though deductible, are not classified as entertainment. As such, these expenses are not subject to the 50% limitation.

Another way to get around the 50% entertainment limit is discussed later in this section under "Business Gifts."

EXAMPLE

Uncle Sammy and Aunt Iris are avid golfers. They go every chance they can. It seems they're almost always dragging some client or potential client with them, including his or her spouse. Afterwards, they all go to the 19th hole, where they quench their thirst, grab a bite to eat, and discuss Sammy's tax business or the client's tax problem. Sammy pays only for his and Aunt Iris's green fees and food. What can Sammy deduct?

If they didn't go to the watering hole after the golf outing, then the golf game would not be deductible unless there was a substantial business discussion at another time during the day. If there were, then the green fees would be deductible but not the mileage. However, since they discussed business after the round of golf, even though over a meal, everything is deductible: the transportation, green fees, cart rental, food, beverages, tips, and taxes. Also, the day's use of the golf clubs is deductible.

AUDIT-PROOFING TECHNIQUES

Once upon a time, if you did not have records to support your entertainment deductions you were allowed to estimate them under the Cohan Rule. However, that's no longer the case. If you get audited, the "guilty until proven innocent rule" applies. If you cannot produce the required documentation, your deduction will be denied.

For all deductions for entertainment, record the following information:

1. The cost of every expense
2. The date of entertainment
3. The name, location, and type of entertainment
4. When and Where the discussion took place, how long it lasted, who participated in it, and their business relationship to you
5. The business reason or the value of the business benefit to be derived or expected to be derived

You should also keep your receipts (or other documentation) for every entertainment expense of $75 or more. It is also recommended, though not required, that you maintain receipts for items costing less than $75.

If you write off any business-related entertaining at your home, you will need to fulfill the same record-keeping requirements as above. You will also find it helpful to have a separate grocery receipt. That is, if you buy food for the week along with the food for your guests, have the clerk put the two kinds of purchases on separate receipts.

Business Gifts

Gifts you give in the course of your trade or business are deductible business expenses. The gift can be given to any person or company who has a business relationship or a potential business relationship to you. The person can even be a family member.

The limitation is $25 per individual recipient. There is no limit on the size of the gift deduction to entities other than individuals. However, if the gift is intended for the personal use or benefit of a particular person or a limited class of people, then the $25 limitation will apply.

Unlike entertainment expenses, business gifts are deductible 100% up to the $25 limit.

> **TIP:** *Here's how to get around the 50% entertainment limitation. Instead of going with your client to the football game or theater, give them the tickets as a gift. Pay for their entertainment, but don't tag along. Since it's a gift, the cost of the tickets will be fully deductible. Once you've reached the $25 for that client, start tagging along. The tickets will now be considered an entertainment expense. The 50% limitation applies, but the $25 gift limitation doesn't apply.*

AUDIT-PROOFING TECHNIQUES

For gifts, you must substantiate:

1. The cost
2. The date you gave the gift
3. A description of the gift
4. The business reason for the gift or the value of the business benefit to be derived or expected to be derived as a result of the gift
5. The occupation or other information related to the recipient, such as the recipient's name and title (The point is that you must show a business relationship.)

▶ **SECTION E: DEDUCTING BUSINESS TRIPS AND VACATIONS**

All ordinary and necessary expenses you pay while traveling away from home on business are deductible. Although these expenses do *not* need to be *indispensable* to your business, they cannot be lavish or extravagant.

There are two categories of business trip expenses:

1. **En-Route Expenses.** These are expenses incurred while going to, and coming home from, your destination. This type of expense typically includes:
   ▶ Airfare, train fare, bus fare
   ▶ Tips
   ▶ Car expenses
   ▶ Meals, beverages, and lodging while en route

2. **At-Destination Expenses.** These are expenses you incur while at your destination. Typical at-destination expenses include:
   ▶ Lodging
   ▶ Local transportation
   ▶ Car rental
   ▶ Meals and beverages
   ▶ Taxes
   ▶ Tips
   ▶ Dry cleaning, laundry, pressing
   ▶ Business telephone calls

Remember! The 50% Entertainment Limitation Applies. The cost of meals and entertainment while away on business are still subject to the 50% entertainment limitation.

EXAMPLES

Here's a short quiz to test you on the material covered in the previous section.

Situation #1. It's April 15, and Uncle Sammy has to work long hours to meet the filing deadline for his client's tax returns. He gets up early in the morning and works nonstop all day. In the evening he takes a short break, grabbing a bite to eat at the local pizza shop. He then goes back to work. Is his dinner deductible?

Situation #2. As you remember, Uncle Sammy lives in Boulder, Colorado. He flies to San Francisco early one morning. There he has an all-day, nonstop business meeting that lasts until early evening. That evening, before returning to Colorado, he grabs a bite to eat at the airport. Is that meal deductible?

Situation #3. Uncle Sammy drives to Denver, which is just twenty miles from his home in Boulder. His meeting lasts till late at night. Being too tired to drive home he grabs a bite to eat and spends the night in a motel. Is the meal in the evening deductible?

The Answers:

Situation #1. Not deductible.

Situation #2. Not deductible.

Situation #3. Deductible.

What's different about #3 that makes it deductible? It qualifies as a business trip! Why isn't Sammy's trip to San Francisco considered a business trip? As will soon be discussed, to qualify your trip as a business expense, you must be away from home overnight. When Uncle Sammy went to San Francisco he came home the same day.

While you are on a business trip, many expenses that wouldn't otherwise be deductible magically turn into a business deduction. When you go away on business, you want to play your cards right to get the biggest tax-saving deductions possible. And if you do play your cards right, you can even turn your vacation into a tax-saving deduction.

Business Trip Defined

What turns a trip into a business deduction? There are very specific requirements that must be satisfied. First, your business duties must require you to be away from your *tax home* substantially longer than a day's work. Secondly, you must be away from home *overnight*. Well, that seems straight forward enough, doesn't it? (Don't forget we're dealing with the Tax Code.)

Home. Isn't that the place I come to after work to kick back on the ol' recliner, crack open a beer, and zone out on the tube? Not necessarily. For purposes of this discussion and to avoid confusion we'll refer to your home as your "tax home."

Your tax home is where your regular or principal place of business is located. If you don't have a regular or principal place of business, your tax home will be your residence. I know that seems like an unnecessary distinction, but not everyone's residence is in the same place as their work.

For example, many Californians have taken refuge in Colorado—there are fewer people, lower taxes, and a much lower cost of living. Some of the Californians, however, don't want to leave their jobs or can't find comparable work in Colorado. So they stay and work in California during the week and return home to Colorado on the weekends. Some even make enough money to commute between California and Colorado daily. For these people, Colorado is their home, but California is their tax home.

Let's put this definition into operation. If your residence and your primary place of business are in the same area, that's where your tax home is. If they're in different locations, your tax home is where you work.

What if you work in California and live in Colorado? Are the traveling costs between these two locations deductible? No, because those are commuting expenses—if you recall, transportation expenses between where you live and where you work are not deductible. But what if, besides California being your principal place of work, you also conducted your business in Colorado? You're still not entitled to a deduction for the cost of travel *unless* your primary motivation for traveling is business related.

If you do have two or more places of work, how do you determine your tax home? There are several factors to consider. The most significant is time spent in each location. Two other factors are the degree of business activity conducted in each place, and the relative significance of the financial return in each area.

By the way, do you think everyone has a tax home?

How about the salesman who travels all around the country and doesn't have a place he calls home? He sleeps in motels and eats in restaurants throughout the country. Since he doesn't have a regular or principal place of business, or a residence, he doesn't have a tax home. Therefore, he doesn't qualify for this deduction: He doesn't have a tax home to be away from.

Overnight. This term is a bit easier to define. If you're away from home substantially longer than an ordinary workday, and while away from home you need a substantial amount of sleep, you are considered to be away overnight. In most situations, if you're away from home for at least one night you meet this qualification.

Traveling to temporary work locations. Don't forget, even if you don't meet these criteria, you can still deduct transportation expenses to and from temporary work locations outside of your normal geographical area of work.

(Please see Part Four, Section C, "Getting the Most 'TSPM' Out of Your Car.")

Factors Affecting the Deduction

After determining whether your travels qualify as a business trip, it's necessary to determine which expenses are deductible and to what extent you can deduct them. There are three factors that affect the amount of deduction you can claim for business trips. These factors are:

1. Whether the trip is **primarily for business** or primarily for non-business purposes
2. Whether the trip is **within the USA** or to a foreign country
3. Whether the expenses are **en-route expenses** or **at-destination expenses**

Traveling within the U.S.A.

100% Business, 100% deductible. If your trip is within the United States, and the trip is 100% business-related, all your en-route expenses and at-destination expenses will be deductible.

Primarily for business. If your trip is primarily for business purposes, you will still be entitled to deduct *all* of your en-route expenses, as well as business related at-destination expenses.

If the trip is not primarily for business, you will not be able to deduct *any* of the en-route expenses. However, you will still be able to deduct your business-related at-destination expenses.

Usually, a trip will be considered primarily for business if there are more *business days* than non-business days.

For example, last winter, Uncle Sammy spent 12 days in Hawaii. Of that time, eight days were spent on business and four days on the beach. Therefore, the trip was primarily for business. As such, all of his expenses getting to and getting home from Hawaii were deductible. Also, he can deduct 66% of the expenses he incurred during his stay in Hawaii.

Business days. You'll be glad to learn that you do not need to spend eight hours working for a-day-away to be considered a business day. In fact, certain days qualify as business days even though you spent the whole day sightseeing or playing in the waves. There are actually five ways for a day to qualify as a business day:

1. **The "four hours plus one minute" rule.** If you work more than one-half of the normal eight-hour day, that day will be considered a business day.

2. **Meeting day.** If you need to be at a particular place, on a particular day, for a particular purpose, that day will be considered a business day. And it doesn't matter how long the activity takes. If on one of Sammy's days in Hawaii, he spent the whole day on the beach, except for an hour at a prearranged meeting, that whole day would count as a business day. However, remember that under the "ordinary and necessary" rule, the meeting must serve a legitimate, bona fide, and relatively substantial business purpose.

▶ **TIP:** *A meeting a day keeps taxes away. Don't plan all your meetings on the same day and over-tax yourself. Spread them out.*

3. **Travel days.** For determining whether a trip is primarily for business or not, all travel days are considered business days. When Sammy went to Hawaii, the first and last day he spent on the beach. Since they were travel days, they counted as business days.

   The "slow boat to China" rule. What if, instead of flying, Sammy took two days to drive to California, and from there he took a three-day cruise to Hawaii? Under the "slow boat to China rule" all five days would be counted as business days. You are not required to take the fastest mode of transportation to get to your destination. However, extra days for non-business related detours do not count as business days.

   Traveling by car. According to at least one recognized tax expert, you can limit yourself to averaging driving three hundred miles a day and still have it count as a business day. So let's say it's nine hundred miles to your destination. You can drive six hundred miles one day, three hundred the next, and one hundred the last, and all three will count as business days. For a single driving day to be counted as a business day you must drive at least three hundred miles.

4. **Work Friday, leave Sunday.** Isn't it a drag to travel to a beautiful part of the country, be cooped up in an

office Monday through Friday, then catch a late-night flight home on Friday? Wouldn't it be nice to be able to spend at least one day taking in the sights? In fact, the IRS and the airlines encourage you to stay the weekend. Airfare is usually substantially less expensive if you travel on the weekend instead of during the week. And if the airfare savings are greater than the extra costs for meals and lodging, then Saturday and Sunday will count as business days. Then you can take in the sights, save money on airfare, and even write off the meals and lodgings for the weekend.

5. **Sandwiched weekend.** Here's another way to take in and write off the sights. If while away you work on Friday and the following Monday, then Saturday and Sunday will also count as business days, as long as the cost of going home and coming back is greater than the cost of staying over. This rule also applies to holidays or other necessary "standby" days.

EXAMPLE

Here's an example of how the business days rules operate. Sammy flew to Hawaii on a Thursday, arriving in time to spend most of the day on the beach. On Friday he had a two-hour prescheduled meeting and spent the rest of the day on the beach. He went sightseeing Saturday and Sunday and worked Monday. The next five days were spent sunning himself and swimming with the dolphins. On day 11 he worked from eight in the morning until noon. Then he went on a business lunch until one. The rest of the day was spent on the beach. On day 12 he spent his last day relaxing on the beach and then flew home.

How many of the 12 days were business days? If you said seven you win a trip to anywhere (compliments of the IRS). The Thursday he arrived in Hawaii and the day he left are business days. Friday is a business day because of the scheduled meeting. Monday is a business day. Since Saturday and Sunday are sandwiched between two work days they also count as business days. And day 11 also counts as a business day since he worked more than four hours. Since more than 50% of the days away are business days, the trip is primarily for business. Therefore, the airfare, as well as the costs of getting to and from the airports, is 100% deductible. The expenses in Hawaii that are related to business will also be deductible. However, don't forget: although the meals are deductible, they're still subject to the 50% entertainment limitation.

What if Uncle Sammy wanted to get as much time relaxing in the sun as possible? Instead of spending five days on the beach he might spend six. And on top of that, he might spend the whole day 12 on the beach. And on day twelve he flew out of Hawaii late at night and arrived at home the next day. According to some authorities, Sammy's trip would still be considered primarily for business. Since he left on day 12 and arrived home the next day, both days would count as business days. Therefore, he would have had seven business days and six non-business days.

Foreign Travel

The rules for deducting expenses related to traveling to foreign countries are different from those for traveling within the United States. However, the definition of a business day is the same.

En-route expenses. If the trip is entirely for business or considered entirely for business then *all* en-route expenses are deductible. Your trip is considered for business if you satisfy any of the following five criteria:

1. **It is 100% business.**

2. **You are outside the U.S.A. for fewer than eight days.** If the trip is primarily for business and lasts fewer than eight days, it will be considered "entirely for business" and you will be able to deduct 100% of the cost of getting to and from your destination. In calculating the number of days, do not start counting until the day after you left the United States. However, do count the day you return.

   For example, Zsa Zsa goes to Paris primarily for business purposes. On day one she flies from Denver to New York. Day two, she flies from New York to Paris. On days three and four she attends business meetings. Days five through eight she spends sightseeing. On day nine she flies back to New York. And on day ten she flies from New York to Denver. Is Zsa Zsa's trip considered entirely for business? Days one and ten do not count toward the days outside the United States because she's still in the country. Day two doesn't count, either, because it's the day of departing from the United States. Days three through nine count; however, they add up to only seven days, and therefore the trip is considered entirely for business and all her traveling expenses while en-route are deductible.

3. **You are outside the U.S.A. more than one week, but spend less than 25% of the time on non-business activities.** If the trip is primarily for business, you spend more than a week outside the United States, and less than 25% of the time is spent on non-business activities, then the trip will be considered entirely for business. The percentage of time spent on business is determined on a per-day basis. Business days are defined as discussed earlier, regarding travel within the USA. For instance, for this purpose, both days of departure and return count as business days.

4. **It is not a personal vacation.** If you can establish that a personal vacation was not a major consideration, the trip will be considered entirely for business and all the en-route expenses will be deductible. By the way, visiting a relative in a hospital is not considered a vacation.

5. **You are not in control.** If you did not have substantial control over arranging the trip, it will be considered entirely for business. However, if you're your own boss, you will be considered as having control.

If the trip is primarily for business, but more than 25% of the time is non-business days, you will need to allocate the en-route expenses. For allocation purposes, both days of departure and return count as business days.

If the trip is not primarily for business, en-route expenses will not be deductible at all.

At-destination expenses. For foreign travel, if the trip is primarily for business, the at-destination expenses must be allocated based on the proportion of business days to total days away. In the example above, Zsa Zsa will not be able to deduct the costs of days five through eight, since they are non-business days. Thus, she would be able to deduct 60% of her costs, since six days out of the ten were business days.

If the trip is not primarily for business, the at-destination expenses will not be deductible. However, direct expenses are deductible. For instance, Zsa Zsa's trip to Paris is not primarily for business; therefore she will not be able to deduct any of the airfare, lodging, or food while away. However, if she attends a seminar directly related to her business, she will be able to deduct the cost of the seminar.

Travel by Sea

If you travel by ocean liner, cruise ship, or other form of luxury water transportation your deduction is limited. But don't worry—it's limited to twice the highest federal *per diem* rate allowed employees of the executive branch. "Federal *per diem*" is the amount the government reimburses its workers for each day the worker is away from home on business.

The following chart shows the applicable rates for 1996.

1996 Dates	Highest Federal *Per Diem*	Daily Limit
January 1–March 31	$204	$408
April 1–April 30	202	404
May 1–May 31	180	360
June 1–October 31	202	404
November 1–December 31	204	408

Conventions, Seminars, and Other Meetings

There are additional limits and requirements for attending conventions, seminars, and other meetings for which you claim a travel deduction.

Within North America (includes Canada, Mexico, and many warm-weather islands). Travel expenses related to attending conventions, seminars, and other meetings within North America are deductible if:

1. The activity benefits your business; and
2. There are at least six hours of scheduled activities; and
3. You attend at least four hours and one minute of the activities

Outside North America. Travel expenses related to attending conventions, seminars, and other meetings outside North America are deductible if:

1. The activity is directly related to your business; and
2. It's as reasonable to hold the activity outside North America as in it; and

3. The travel expenses qualify as a deduction under the Foreign Travel rules.

Cruise ships. You can deduct, up to $2,000 per year, the expenses of attending conventions, seminars, or other similar meetings held on cruise ships (or any other ship that sails) if:

1. The meeting is directly related to your business; and
2. The ship is a vessel registered in the United States; and
3. All of the ship's ports of call are located in the United States or its possessions, and
4. You attach the required documents to your tax return.

AUDIT-PROOFING TECHNIQUES

Well, we once again have to address the topic most of us like even less than taxes: keeping records. When you're traveling, be sure to record the following:

1. The amount of each expense
2. The dates of departure and return for each trip away from home, including days away from home spent on business.
3. Where you went
4. The business reasons or nature of the business-benefit derived or expected to be derived as a result of the travel

You also need the receipts for items costing $75 or more—unless they're not readily available, such as for phone, tips, and cabs. If you don't have a receipt, be sure you make a record of the expense anyway.

As a self-employed taxpayer, you may elect to use standard *per diem* rates for meals and incidental expenses. The advantage of using the standard rates is that you don't need receipts to prove these expenses. If your actual costs for meals and incidentals, such as the cost of laundry, cleaning, and maid tips, are less than the standard *per diem* rate, you definitely want to use the standard rates.

The *per diem* election is not available to employees related to the employer. This prohibition includes spouses, children, and 10%-or-more shareholders of an S Corporation (see Part Seven).

The meal-allowance rate for 1997 was $30 each day in most areas of the country. For certain specified areas in the country, the rate may be $30, $34, $38, or $42, depending on where you travel. (Please see Appendix C for locations eligible for higher allowances.) For locations outside the continental USA, the rates are updated monthly. Call 202-512-1800 for specific information.

If you are not traveling for an entire 24-hour day, you must prorate the standard meal allowance. For instance, if you leave on a business trip at noon, then, you would be entitled to one-half of that day's meal allowance. If you arrive home from a business trip at 6 P.M., then for that day you would be allowed 75% of the meal allowance.

Take Your Spouse with You

If your spouse, or for that matter anyone else, is your employee, and there is a legitimate business purpose for that person to go on the trip with you, your business can pay for and deduct that other person's expenses as well as your own.

What if your non-employee spouse goes with you? His or her expenses are not deductible. Does that mean that if a single room costs $60 a night and a double costs $72, you can only deduct $36 for the night? No, you still get to deduct the amount you would have been entitled to if you were alone. In this case, you may still deduct $60 a night for lodging. Likewise, if you drive to your business destination, take along your spouse, your kids, and your dog. The automobile costs will be 100% deductible.

Don't forget, if you have a legitimate business entertainment, the cost of your spouse is deductible—if you entertain clients while away on business and bring your spouse along, you will still be able to deduct your spouse's share of the entertainment.

Turning Your Vacation into a Tax-Saving Deduction

You've worked the whole year. Now you're ready to unwide, relax, and let yourself calm down. It's time to go on your vacation. Instead of winding down and relaxing, you get more uptight because of the cost. You need to get away, but you can't really afford it.

If you play your cards right, you can eat your cake and have it, too. That is, you can go on your vacation at a reduced rate by turning your vacation into a tax-saving deduction, and let the IRS pay for part of the trip. Here's how it works. Go to a place where you can conduct your business in some way. Since you need to show you had a business purpose prior to leaving for the trip, make contacts and arrangements before leaving. Spend four hours a day in places that in some way can be connected to your business, and do something business related. Make business contacts. Hand out and collect business cards. Record what you discussed and with whom. If possible, show what income you generated or in what ways your business derived a benefit from the trip.

Remember, if you bring along your spouse or child, be sure they are employees and have a business purpose for accompanying you on the trip, so you can deduct the cost of taking them with you.

▶ SECTION F: CONVERTING MEDICAL AND DENTAL EXPENSES INTO BUSINESS DEDUCTIONS

I'm sure I don't have to tell you about the high cost of health insurance. If you have coverage, the cost is probably making a big dent in your budget. For some the cost might be prohibitive. What's more, most health insurance policies do not cover all our medical expenses. Most Americans are caught between making too much money to be eligible for government assistance and making too little money to afford full health coverage. If you have high medical expenses plus other itemized deductions, you might get a limited tax break. Otherwise, unless you're self-employed, forget about getting any assistance. Luckily, for most self-employed individuals there are ways to convert your medical and dental expenses into business deductions.

Expenses covered in this section:

- ▶ Health-insurance premiums
- ▶ Dental care
- ▶ Health insurance deductible
- ▶ Prescriptions
- ▶ Eyeglasses and contact lenses
- ▶ Pre-existing conditions
- ▶ Childbirth
- ▶ Alternative health care
- ▶ Cost of traveling to and from medical treatment
- ▶ All other out-of-pocket, unreimbursed medical and dental expenses

For most people the tax law does not help make the cost of medical care more affordable. In general, unreimbursed medical expenses are deductible only as an itemized deduction. And you only get a tax benefit if your itemized deductions are more than the allowed standard deduction. And what's more, even then your medical expenses give you a tax benefit *only* to the extent that they exceed 7.5% of your adjusted gross income. Without getting into all the gory details, this deduction probably doesn't do you much good, if any.

The 40% Benefit for the Self-Employed

If you're self-employed, Congress created a tax benefit just for you. It's small, but it's something. Whether or not you itemize your deductions, self-employed business owners are entitled to deduct a portion of their health-insurance premiums. However, the deduction only reduces your federal, state, and local income taxes. It is not a business deduction and therefore does not reduce your self-employment, Social Security, or Medicare taxes.

In 1996, the portion you were able to deduct was 30% of your health-insurance premiums. This rate increases to 40% in 1997, and will continue going up, reaching 100% in the year 2007.

DEDUCTIBLE HEALTH INSURANCE CHART	
1995	25%
1996	30%
1997	40%
1998–1999	45%
2000–2001	50%
2002	60%
2003–2005	80%
2006	90%
2007 & after	100%

These deductions help a little, but only a very little. For example, let's say Uncle Sammy, in 1997, paid $200 each month for his family's health insurance and an additional $1,000 for out-of-pocket medical expenses. Given our basic assumptions of Sammy's combined federal and state income tax of 33%, his tax savings on the medical expenses of $3,400 would be only $316.80. By the end of this section, you will learn how Sammy's tax savings related to health insurance can be increased by almost 500%.

The 100% Tax Benefit for the Self-Employed

If you're self-employed there are ways to deduct *all* your medical and dental expenses. You do not have to be limited to the itemized deduction rules or the piddling tax savings from the health-insurance deduction. And what's more, these expenses will be business deductions. Thus, your self-employment, Social Security, and Medicare taxes will be reduced as well as your income taxes.

Turning Health Insurance into a 100% Business Deduction

In general, health-insurance coverage provided for employees is deductible by the employer and not taxable to the employee. However, unless your business is a C Corporation, the cost of a health-insurance policy for yourself is not a business deduction. As will be discussed in greater detail in Part Seven, a C Corporation is a business that is incorporated and whose shareholders do not elect for it to be treated as an S Corporation, in which the company's profits and losses pass through to the shareholders and are included on the shareholders' income tax returns.

Even if your business is not a C Corporation, there is a way for the business to pay for your health insurance, for the business to write it off, and for you not have to include it as part of your taxable income. However, you have to be married. If you're married, you can hire your spouse as an employee. Have your business provide health insurance for your employee-spouse and have your spouse elect family coverage. If you do that, your spouse will be covered, your spouse's children will be covered, and your spouse's spouse (guess who that is?) will be covered. And what's more, the cost of the health insurance will be a business deduction and not taxable to your employee-spouse. Even if you have other employees you can discriminate. That means you can elect to provide health-insurance coverage for any particular class or classes of employees.

The health-insurance coverage must be provided for in a written plan and the policy fee must be billed to the business. Also, the cost of the insurance must be reasonable with respect to the employee's salary. And that employee's total remuneration, including the cost of the health insurance, must be reasonable with respect to the work performed. (See Part Six.)

> **NOTE:** This technique is *not* available to partnerships or shareholders of S Corporations owning 2% or more of the corporation's stock. S Corporations, as will be discussed in Part Seven, are incorporated businesses whose shareholders elect to be treated as partnerships for tax purposes while retaining the limited-liability feature of a corporation.

What if you're not married? For an unmarried business owner to get a business deduction for the cost of his or her health insurance, the business must be a C Corporation. Shareholder-employees of C Corporations are treated as any other employee. As such, they're entitled to receive the same benefits all other employees are entitled to. And this is true even if the shareholder-employee is the only employee of the company. So if you're not married and you want to receive a business deduction for the cost of your health insurance, incorporate your business and provide coverage for yourself through the business.

Turning All Other Medical and Dental Expenses into Business Deductions

It's great to be able to convert your health insurance into a business deduction. Unfortunately, health insurance rarely covers all our medical costs. Typical unreimbursed, out-of-pocket expenses include the deductible on your insurance policy, eyeglasses, dental care, pre-existing conditions, and alternative health care. But you can have your business pay for these expenses tax free. Here's how you can do it.

If you're married, hire your spouse and adopt a medical and dental reimbursement plan. This plan will entitle you to pay for each of your employees' unreimbursed out-of-pocket medical and dental expenses. As with insurance, if the plan provides family coverage for the employees, then your employee-spouse's immediate family, including you, will be covered.

Also, as with the health insurance, this is not available to partnerships or shareholders owning 2% or more of an S Corporation. And if you're not married, you will have to resort to a C Corporation.

There are specific criteria you will need to satisfy in order to rest assured that your health-insurance and medical reimbursements satisfy ERISA (Employee Retirement Income Security Act) rules and IRS requirements. There are companies that for a nominal fee will do all the necessary paperwork for you and guarantee their work. One such company is BIZPLAN. See Resource Guide in Appendix F for information on how to contact them.

▶ **WATCH OUT!** *Medical reimbursement plans must be provided for all eligible employees. You cannot limit coverage to a certain class of employees as you can with health-insurance coverage.*

▶ **TIP:** *Is the net profit from your sole proprietorship or wages from your C Corporation greater than the amount subject to the Social Security tax? If so, you might be subjecting income to the Social Security tax (12.4%) that would not otherwise be, in which case you will need to weigh the benefit against the cost. For example, if in 1997 Uncle Sammy's net profit was $80,000, only $65,400 of that would be subject to the Social Security portion of the self-employment tax. However, if he reduces the next profit $10,000 by paying that amount to Aunt Iris as salary, then $75,400 would be subject to the Social Security tax instead of $65,400: the $65,400 limit, plus the $10,000 of Aunt Iris's salary, is considered separately.*

NOTE: Wages paid to spouses are subject to payroll taxes. The less you pay your spouse the lower your payroll taxes will be. However, you must still pay your spouse a reasonable wage or salary. Please see Part Six for the definition of *"reasonable wage or salary."*

Medical Savings Account

You might have heard about the "medical savings account" (MSA). This is a new device created to encourage employers to provide health insurance to their employees. However, it is really more related to retirement than to converting medical expenses into business deductions. Therefore, it is covered in Part Six, "Choosing the Best Retirement Plan for You."

Disability Insurance

Don't confuse health insurance and disability insurance. The latter compensates for *loss of income* due to sickness or accident.

In general, your business will be able to deduct the cost of disability premiums paid on behalf of your employees. If the premium is included in your employee's taxable income, then any benefits received by your employee through the policy will be tax-free. On the other hand, if the premiums are tax-free to the employee, then benefits are not.

As with health insurance, the disability premiums paid on your own behalf are not deductible to the business, unless the business is organized as a C Corporation. However, since the premiums are not tax-free, any benefits received through the policy will be.

Planning Tip! Hire your spouse and pay your employee-spouse's disability premium. The premium will be tax-deductible to the business and tax-free to the employee-spouse. However, if you expect your spouse to become disabled, then pay for the premium personally. Then the premium won't be deductible, but the benefits will be tax-free.

CALCULATE YOUR TAX SAVINGS

1. Health Insurance Premiums $ _____

2. Out-of-Pocket Medical Expenses $ _____

3. Total Medical Expenses (Line 1 + Line 2) $ _____

Tax Rates:

4. Federal Income   . _____

5. State and Local Income   . _____

6. Self-Employment   . _____

7. Total Tax Rate (Lines 4 + 5 + 6) . _____

8. Line 3 × Line 7 $ _____

If You Do Not Use Itemized Deductions, Skip to Line 10.

9. a. Total Medical Expenses (Line 3) $ _____

    b. Adjusted Gross Income
        $ _____ × .075 $ _____

    c. Medical Itemized Deduction
        (Line 9a − Line 9b) $ _____

10. Health Insurance Premium
    (Line 1) × .30 $ _____

11. Line 9c + Line 10 $ _____

12. Income Tax Rate (Line 4 + Line 5)   . _____

13. Line 11 × Line 12 $ _____

14. YOUR TAX SAVINGS (Line 8 − Line 13) $ _____

AUDIT-PROOFING TECHNIQUES

Let's face it: hiring your spouse can save you a lot in taxes—so naturally the IRS thinks there might be a temptation to take advantage of these tax-saving deductions without your spouse doing any real work for you. Therefore, you have to be prepared during an audit to prove you are entitled to the deduction. You must be able to substantiate that the amount you paid your spouse was for services actually rendered. Here's what to do:

1. Make a written employment agreement between your business and your spouse. The agreement should contain a description of the services to be rendered, the amount of compensation, the fringe benefits, and when the agreement begins and when it ends. Both of you should sign it. (Please see the sample employment agreement printed in Appendix D).

2. Make sure your spouse fills out all required employment forms, such as Form W-4.

3. Provide your spouse and the government with *timely* filed W-2s.

4. File all other employment-related forms with the federal, state, and local governments in a *timely* manner.

5. Make sure your spouse fills out time cards.

6. Pay your spouse at regular intervals and on time.

7. Make sure your spouse qualifies as an employee and not as an independent contractor. (See the discussion in Part Two, Section B, on independent contractors versus employees.)

TAX-SAVING STEPS YOU CAN TAKE TODAY

HIRE YOUR SPOUSE

☐ Write an employment agreement. Make sure it contains:
  ☐ A description of any services to be performed
  ☐ The amount of compensation
  ☐ The fringe benefits
  ☐ The time period the agreement covers
  ☐ Both your and your spouse's signatures

☐ Have your spouse fill out a W-4 Form.

☐ Have your spouse fill out time cards.

☐ Pay your spouse at regular intervals and on time.

☐ File all government-employee related documents in a timely manner.

SET UP A HEALTH-CARE PLAN

☐ Hire your spouse

☐ Adopt a medical reimbursement plan for your business. Make sure it's in writing.

☐ Have your business purchase a health-insurance policy on behalf of your spouse and all your spouse's family, including you.

▶ **SECTION G: CLOTHING, INTEREST, CREDIT CARDS, RAISING CHILDREN, AND EVERYTHING ELSE**

Clothing

After graduating from law school I worked for a firm that required its employees to wear three-piece suits. To let you know a little about myself—I'm secretly a rebel. I hate collars that touch and irritate my neck, and any kind of noose around my neck—like a tie, or any other unnecessary garment draped over my body. I only bought and wore a three-piece suit because it was required. Now I work for myself. Believe me, there is not even one piece of a three-piece suit in my closet.

However, back then I had to wear it for my job. Was it deductible? Remember Internal Revenue Code Section 162, "all ordinary & necessary expenses paid or incurred during the taxable year"? The suit was ordinary, and I was required to wear it for my livelihood so it was necessary. But, clothing is deductible as a business expense only if it is "(1) specifically required as a condition of employment **and** (2) not of a type adaptable to general or continued usage to the extent that it takes the place of regular clothing."

I passed the first criteria. But what about the second one, "take the place of regular clothing"? As far as I was concerned it didn't take the place of my blue jeans, which was the only thing I considered regular clothing. Unfortunately, it's not a subjective test. That means it doesn't matter what I thought of the three-piece suit. For many other people a three-piece suit might be regular social attire. I lost. No deduction.

If you wear clothing or a uniform that wouldn't normally be worn outside of the work environment, then it will be deductible—for example, painter's overalls, steel-toed construction worker's boots, or an astronaut suit.

Turning clothing into a business deduction. There is a way to convert your everyday clothing into a business deduction. If you affix your logo or business name to an article of clothing, it will be deductible. The logo must be premanently affixed; clipping on a nametag will not do. And it must be visible, so don't bother monogramming your underwear.

I'll bet some of you are thinking, "I'm not going to put my logo or business name on my clothing; that's too tacky." Next time you go outside, count the number of people wearing other people's names on their clothing: Eddie Bauer, Yves Saint Laurent, or whoever. Not only do these companies charge extra to give us the privilege of wearing their names on our chests, we're also free walking billboards for them.

Why pay extra to advertise somebody else's business? You may as well advertise your own business and write off your clothing at the same time. By the way, wearing your business name on your shirt is a great way to market your business. Wherever you are, you're effectively marketing yourself without even having to say a word.

Interest

All interest used to be deductible. Now it's limited only to:

- ▶ Home mortgage interest
- ▶ Investment interest
- ▶ Business interest
- ▶ Student-loan interest (beginning in 1998, interest on student loans is deductible, with limitations)

Most Americans pay a lot of interest that's not deductible, such as the interest on credit cards and college loans.

You can save a lot of these costs if you convert your personal debt to a business debt. That way you're able to deduct your personal interest and reduce your taxes.

One way to do this is to pay off your non-business debts before you pay your business debts. If you borrow money to live on, instead borrow money to run your business.

If you take out a loan for your business, it's best if you put the loan proceeds into your business account. If you put the money into your personal account, you run the risk of having the IRS claim that the funds were used for personal purposes, and it will deny the interest deduction. If you don't put the money into your business account, then put it in a separate account, or spend it for the purpose for which it was intended within 30 days.

It is also a good idea to use three different credit cards: one for personal expenditures, a second for business purchases, and the third for expenses related to your automobile. Try to pay off the personal one prior to the expiration of the grace period so it doesn't accrue interest. The interest and credit-card fee on the business credit card will be 100% deductible. And the interest and credit-card fee on the third one will be deductible to the extent that your car is used for business purposes, even if you take the standard deduction.

Converting the Costs of Raising Your Child

In general, the costs related to supporting your child, such as allowance, food, shelter, clothing, and weddings, are not deductible. However, there are a several income-shifting techniques you can use to convert these expenses into business deductions. These techniques involve hiring your child, giving an ownership interest in your business as a gift to your child, or giving equipment as a gift to your child and having the business lease it back. All these techniques are fully discussed in Part Five.

All Other Everyday Living Expenses

There probably are some living expenses you have that were not specifically covered. That doesn't mean they're not convertible into a business deduction. Remember,

EVERYTHING YOU DO, EVERYWHERE YOU GO, AND EVERYONE YOU MEET CAN BE RELATED TO YOUR BUSINESS.

And if an expense pertains to an activity or thing related to your business, then it's deductible, as long as it's ordinary and necessary. However, be sure you have the substantiation necessary to support the deduction you claimed.

INCOME-SHIFTING
TECHNIQUES

Is the cost of raising your child expensive? How would you like the following costs of raising a child to reduce your taxes?

- ▶ Allowance
- ▶ Music lessons
- ▶ Computer
- ▶ Food
- ▶ Clothing
- ▶ College education
- ▶ Wedding

Do you help your parents or anyone else out financially? Would you like to ease your financial burden by being able to reduce your taxes with *those* payments?

For most people, the only help they get is by being able to claim some people they support as dependents. For each dependent you claim you receive a deduction called a "Personal Exemption." In 1997, the personal exemption was $2,650. However, that deduction applies only against your income tax, not your Social Security or Medicare taxes. And for you to be able to claim someone you support as a dependent, three tests must be satisfied.

If you own your own business, you can effectively receive tax relief for these costs. By using one of the income-shifting techniques, you will be able to shift income that would be taxed at your tax bracket to your child, parent, or anyone else who is in a lower tax bracket. The results of doing this are:

1. Your child, parent, or whoever receives the money you would have spent on their behalf.
2. That money is not included in your taxable income.
3. That money is still subject to taxation, but at the recipient's tax rate.
4. The government receives less tax on that amount of money.
5. If they qualified as your dependent before, they will still qualify as long as you continue to provide more than half their support each year.

We will discuss the following four easy-to-use income-shifting techniques:

▶ Hiring family or friends
▶ Gift ownership of business
▶ Lease property from family or friends
▶ Gift appreciated property

But before discussing these income-shifting techniques, we must provide you with a few tax basics.

The standard deduction. Everyone filing an income-tax return is entitled to a standard deduction. The standard deduction reduces the amount of income subject to the income tax. The amount of standard deduction you're entitled to depends on your filing status, whether someone else can claim you as a dependent, your age, whether you are blind, and your earned income. For the purposes of the following discussions it will be necessary to know a few rules about the standard deduction.

1. For individuals whose filing status was "single" in 1997 the standard deduction was $4,150.
2. For individuals who can be claimed as a dependent on someone else's tax return, the standard deduction is the greater of $650 or their earned income, but not more than $4,150. In 1998, this changes to the greater of $500 or the dependent's earned income plus $250, but is not to exceed $4,150.
3. These deductions are increased for taxpayers who are at least 65 years old or blind.

Personal Exemptions. In addition to the standard deduction, your personal exemption further reduces the amount of income subject to the income tax. You are allowed a personal exemption for yourself and each of your dependents. However, if you are claimed as a dependent on another's tax return, you are not allowed an exemption for yourself on your own tax return. As of 1997, for each exemption claimed there was allowed a $2,650 deduction.

> ▶ **INCOME-SHIFTING TECHNIQUE #1: HIRING**

One effective way to shift income to children, parents, other relatives, or friends is by hiring them to do work for your business. Your business will be able to deduct the amount you pay them; however, it will be included in *their* taxable income.

EXAMPLE

Let's say Sammy hired his 19-year-old son, Fred, and paid him $4,000 for the year. Since that was Fred's only source of income that year, he will not pay any income tax on that money. That's because he's able to reduce his income by the $4,150 standard deduction. Had Sammy not had that business expense, he would have paid income taxes of 33% on that $4000. As a result of Fred's working for Uncle Sammy's business, the family saves $1320 in income taxes.

But aren't Fred's wages subject to Social Security and Medicare taxes? Sure they are. However, if Sammy had not paid the $4,000 to Fred, Sammy would have paid just about the same amount of Social Security and Medicare taxes on that money. Therefore, that's a wash.

Payroll taxes. The amount paid to another individual in the form of wages or salary is subject to payroll taxes. This includes FICA, federal, and state unemployment insurance, and workers' compensation. The monies paid a worker who is hired as an independent contractor are not subject to payroll taxes, but are subject to the self-employment tax. In most situations, the additional payroll or self-employment tax is minimal. That's because if you had not hired the other person, the amount you paid them would have been included in your income and subject to most of those taxes anyway.

▶ **WATCH OUT!** *If your earned income exceeds the Social Security tax limit, your tax savings from hiring someone else can be greatly diminished. That's because you're transferring income that to you would not be subject to the Social Security tax, but to the other person will be. In 1997 the Social Security tax rate was 12.4%, and the taxable ceiling was $65,400.*

Also, if you hire anyone over 65 years old, be careful not to pay them more than they're entitled to without affecting their Social Security benefits. If this is an issue, it would be better to shift income to them using one of the other income-shifting techniques. Only earned income can reduce Social Security benefits. Income from passive sources such as dividends and rental income do not affect your Social Security benefits.

Hiring children under eighteen years old. The biggest tax saving from hiring someone else can result when you hire children. In certain situations, wages or salaries paid to children are exempt from *all* payroll taxes. To qualify for this exemption, you must satisfy all the following criteria:

1. The child must be under 18 years old, and
2. The child must be an employee (not an independent contractor), and

3. The child must be employed by his or her own parent, and

4. The parent's business must be a sole proprietorship.

If, in the above example, Sammy's son Fred were 17 years old, the family would have saved an additional $520. If Fred were under 18, the $4000 Sammy paid him would have saved the family a total of $1840.

AUDIT-PROOFING TECHNIQUES

As you can see, there are potentially great tax savings available when you employ family members. The IRS knows this. So especially when hiring your child, make sure you audit-proof this deduction.

Legitimate business function. The person working for you must serve a legitimate function related to your business. They can perform tasks as simple as licking envelopes, as long as it fulfills a need of your business. If you have children, consider things they're already doing, such as cleaning the office, answering the phone, washing your car, or doing computer input. Instead of giving them allowances, pay them salaries.

Reasonable salary. Make sure you pay the person you're employing a reasonable salary. The amount you pay will be considered reasonable if it is not more than what would normally be paid someone else for doing the same kind of work, at the same level of efficiency and quality.

Age. When hiring someone, be sure not to violate your state's child labor laws with regard to minimum age. In many states you cannot employ someone under the age of

16. However, in most states, if not all, parents hiring their own children are exempt from the minimum-age requirement, unless they're engaged in activities deemed hazardous.

In several cases, the IRS has challenged parents' deducting wages paid to their children, on the grounds the child was too young to be performing any legitimate business function. Perhaps they didn't know that Mozart was composing symphonies before he was five years old. In one case the courts ruled that seven was not too young. It's possible your child can be performing a legitimate business function at a younger age. Each case is decided on its own merits.

Employment agreement. As when hiring your spouse, draw up an employment agreement. The agreement should contain a description of the services to be rendered, the amount of compensation, the fringe benefits, the beginning date, and the ending date. (Please see Appendix D for a sample employment agreement.) If you are hiring the worker as an independent contractor, draw up an independent-contractor agreement. (Please see Appendix B for a sample independent-contractor agreement.)

Employment forms. Make sure all required federal and state employment forms are filled out and filed in a timely way. Some of the required federal employment forms include Forms W-4, W-2, W-3, 941, and 940. If you are hiring the worker as an independent contractor, be sure to file Form 1099-MISC.

Time cards. Make sure your employee fills out a time card. It should include the date, hours worked, and nature of the work performed.

CALCULATE YOUR TAX SAVINGS

1. Annual Wages Paid to the Worker $ _____

2. Your Federal Income-Tax
    Rate   . _____

3. Your State Income-Tax Rate   . _____

4. Your Self-Employment Tax
    Rate   . _____

    (Note: Remember $65,400 Upper
    Limit for 1997)
    (See Note on Page 12)

5. Your Total Tax Rate
    (Lines 2 + 3 + 4)   . _____

6. Your Tax Saving (Line 5 × Line 1) $ _____

7a. Worker's Standard Deduction $ _____
    ($4,150 in 1997 if Filing as Single)

7b. Worker's Exemption
    ($2,650 in 1997) $ _____

8. Worker's IRA Contribution $ _____

9. Worker's Deduction
    (Lines 7a + 7b + 8) $ _____

10. Worker's Taxable Income
    (Line 1 − Line 9) $ _____

11. Worker's Federal Income-Tax Rate . _____

12. Worker's State Income-Tax Rate   . _____

13. Worker's FICA Tax (zero if your child
    is under 18)   . _____

14. Worker's Total Tax Rate
    (Line 11 + 12 + 13)   . _____

15. Worker's Tax (Line 1 × Line 14) $ _____

    TAX SAVINGS (Line 6 − Line 15) $ _____

TAX-SAVING STEPS YOU CAN TAKE TODAY
HIRE YOUR FAMILY MEMBERS AND FRIENDS

- Write an employment agreement. Make sure it contains
  —A description of the services to be performed
  —The amount of compensation
  —The fringe benefits
  —The time period the agreement covers
  —The signatures of both you and the family member
- Have the family member fill out a W-4 Form.
- Have the family member fill out time cards.
- Pay the family member at regular intervals and on time.
- File all government-employee-related documents in a timely manner.

Regular pay. Pay the worker at regular intervals and on time.

Separate bank account. If you employ your child, he or she should have a separate bank account. Also, you should pay your child by check and he or she should deposit it in that account. In that way you will have a paper trail proving you actually paid your child.

Do not hire as an independent contractor. Although it is usually beneficial to hire a worker as an independent contractor, this is not the case if you're a sole proprietor hiring your child who is under 18 years old. To get the best tax benefit, treat the child as an employee and make sure he or she fits the classification of an employee.

▶ INCOME-SHIFTING TECHNIQUE #2: GIFT OWNERSHIP

Another effective way to shift income to another person—family or friend—in a lower tax bracket is by transferring an interest in your business to them. As part-owners of the business, they're entitled to a percentage of the profits equal to the percent of the business they own. This effectively shifts income from you to others. Instead of it being taxed at your tax bracket, it's taxed at theirs. This technique is generally most effective for businesses that choose the S Corporation form of entity.

S Corporations. This technique works great for S Corporations. In fact, many business owners organize their business as an S Corporation specifically for this benefit. As will be discussed in greater detail in Part Seven, the profit and loss of S Corporations generally pass through to its shareholders. The corporation does not pay a tax on the profits. Rather, the shareholders include the profit as part of their taxable income on their individual return. The amount received is treated as a dividend, and as such is subject to income tax but not payroll tax.

EXAMPLE

Let's say Uncle Sammy's son Fred's living expenses are about $9,000 each year. Sammy, in order to support his son, organizes his business as an S Corporation. He gives his son, Fred, 50% of the stock ownership. At the end of the first year, the corporation's profit, after Uncle Sammy's salary, is $20,000. Sammy's and Fred's share of the profits will be $10,000 each. If Fred is claimed by Sammy as a dependent,

Fred's tax on his share of $10,000 will be $1,870. Uncle Sammy's tax will be $3,333. Their combined tax on the $20,000 profit from the business is $5,203, computed as follows in the chart below.

If Uncle Sammy didn't give Fred a portion of the business, but instead directly paid for Fred's financial support, the tax on the $20,000 profit would be $6,600. That's an extra $1,397. See chart below.

C Corporations. This technique does not work for businesses organized as C Corporations. That's because, as you

---

FRED'S TAX

1. Dividend Income		$10,000
2. Less: Standard Deduction		− 650
3. Taxable Income		$ 9,350
4. Federal Tax Rate	.15	
5. Colorado Tax Rate	.05	
6. Total Tax Rate		.20
Total Tax (Line 3 × Line 6)		$ 1,870

SAMMY'S TAX (On the Dividend Distribution)

1. Dividend Income		$10,000
2. Federal Tax Rate	.28	
3. Colorado Tax Rate	.05	
4. Total Tax Rate		.33
Total Tax (Line 1 × Line 4)		$ 3,333

Fred's and Uncle Sammy's Combined Tax on the $20,000 Dividend: $5,203

SAMMY'S TAX
(On the Dividend Distribution)

1. Dividend Income		$20,000
2. Federal Tax Rate	.28	
3. Colorado Tax Rate	.05	
4. Total Tax Rate		.33
Total Tax (Line 1 × Line 4)		$ 6,600

---

will learn in Part Seven, C Corporations are taxed on their profits. And if profits are distributed to shareholders in the form of dividends they are again taxed, this time at the shareholder's tax rate. This double taxation is one of the main reasons business owners do not choose the C Corporation as their form of entity.

▶ **WATCH OUT!** *This technique may not work if at the end of the tax year your child is under 14 years old. That's because of the "kiddie tax." If a child under the age of 14 receives passive income in excess of a certain amount ($1,300 for 1997), then a portion of the investment income may be taxed at the child's parent's tax rate. And corporate dividend distributions are considered investment income for this purpose.*

> ## ► INCOME-SHIFTING TECHNIQUE #3:
> ## LEASE PROPERTY FROM FAMILY OR FRIENDS

Another way to shift income to a relative or friend in a lower tax bracket is by leasing property from them. The property can be an office, storage space, warehouse, or any equipment to be used in your business. You get a business deduction. They get rental income.

Let's say Uncle Sammy leases office equipment, including a computer and printer, from Fred for $300 per month. Uncle Sammy would have a $3,600 business deduction for the year and Fred would have $3,600 rental income. The lease payments would reduce Sammy's self-employment tax in addition to his federal and state income taxes, for a tax savings of $1,656.

Assuming the computer was already fully depreciated, Fred would have income of $3,600. As long as Fred is not in the rental business, the income will be subject only to income tax, not self-employment tax. If that were his only source of income, he would pay tax on $2,950 ($3,600 − $650). The tax would be $590 ($2,950 × .2). That's a savings for the family of $1,066 ($1,655 − $590).

Rental activity not a business. As long as the rental or lease activity is not considered a business, the income from it will not be subject to the self-employment tax. In order for the activity to avoid being considered a business, the lessor should not hold him- or herself out as being engaged in a leasing business. They can accomplish this by leasing to only one business and not conducting themselves like a business. For instance, they shouldn't look for additional clients or have business cards and stationery.

▶ **WATCH OUT!** *As with the dividends received from a corporation, rental and lease income are considered passive income. Therefore, if you employ this technique with your under-14-year-old child, a portion of the payments may be taxed at your tax bracket.*

Transferring ownership. In order to take advantage of this technique, the person you're leasing the property from must own it. If you own the property to be leased, you need to transfer it to the other person. The best way to accom-

UNCLE SAMMY'S TAX SAVINGS

Rent Expense	$3,600
Tax Bracket	46%
Tax Saving	$1,656

FRED'S TAX

Rental Income		$3,600
Available Standard Deduction		650
Taxable Income		$2,950
Federal Tax Rate	.15	
State Tax Rate	.05	
Total Income-Tax Rate		.20
Tax on Rental Income		$ 590
FAMILY'S TAX SAVINGS		**$1,066**

plish this is to give it to them as a gift and lease it back. This type of arrangement is known as the gift/leaseback. If you have not purchased the property yet, you can gift the other person with the money to purchase the property. However, this last method usually does not give you the best tax savings, because you lose the benefit of deducting the full cost in the year of purchase allowed under the Section 179 deduction. (See Part Four, Section B, for a discussion of the Section 179 deduction.)

Gift tax. Throughout the following discussions keep in mind these gift-tax rules:

1. The recipient is never taxed on the gift he or she receives.
2. Every year you can give away, without any gift-tax consequences, up to $10,000 per recipient. If you're married, you and your spouse together are entitled to give away up to $20,000 each year, per recipient. However, in the latter situation you will need to file a joint tax return reporting gifts in excess of $10,000.
3. Corporations are not permitted to gift property.

The Gift/Leaseback Method

The gift/leaseback method is simple. You gift the property to be leased to the person you'll be leasing it from. You get a business deduction and the lessor has rental income. The tax savings are as described above. however, there are a few pointers you should note.

Valid business reason. If your gift/leaseback arrangement is with someone related to you, like your child, you will need to establish a valid business reason for the arrangement—other than tax avoidance. It is recommended to get a letter from a lawyer stating that the gift/leaseback is to accomplish one of the following:

► Protect the asset from creditors
► Avoid conflicts of interest
► Provide for professional management
► Avoid estate-tax probate

Kiddie tax. As discussed above, if the lessor is under 14 years old, your tax savings may be reduced by the kiddie tax.

Trust. If the gift/leaseback is made to your minor child (under 18 years old), it may be necessary to set up a trust and gift the property to the trust.

Gift fully depreciated property. The best property to give as a gift is fully depreciated property. If you own it, you no longer get a depreciation deduction. By gifting and leasing it back, you create a deduction where none existed. For example, let's say your business car is fully depreciated. Its fair market value is $7,000. Its lease value is $2,000 for each of the next four years. Since it's fully depreciated, you would no longer have that deduction. By gifting it and renting it back, you will be able to deduct $2,000 each year. Assuming your tax bracket is 46% your tax savings is $920 each year. However, be sure you hold onto equipment long enough to avoid having to recapture part or all of the depreciation and Section 179 deduction you previously took on that particular equipment.

Three-party leases. In a few states the gift/leaseback arrangements between two parties are not recognized. In these states, you will not be able to just give property as a gift to your child and have your sole proprietorship lease it back. Instead, you will need to create a third party by incorporating your business and having the corporation lease it from your child, so the property to be leased goes from you to your child to your corporation. Check with an attorney to see if this applies in your state.

AUDIT-PROOFING TECHNIQUES

If you employ one of these leasing techniques to shift income to someone else in a lower tax bracket be sure to do the following:

- ▶ Have a written lease, signed by both parties.
- ▶ Pay the fair rental value. (Check with local merchants that rent used equipment to find out the rental value.)
- ▶ Pay the rent by check and on time.
- ▶ The lessor should deposit the rent check in his or her bank account.
- ▶ The lessor must have control of the property. You can enter into a long-term lease agreement ensuring your continued use of the property. However, short-term leases usually command higher rents.

▶ **INCOME-SHIFTING TECHNIQUE #4:**
GIFT PROPERTY INSTEAD OF SELLING

In general, capital assets sold for a gain will be subject to the capital-gains tax. The tax rate on capital assets varies, depending on when you sold the asset, how long you held on to it, and your federal income-tax bracket. The gain is computed by deducting your adjusted basis in the property from the sales price. In general, the adjusted basis is your cost less depreciation and the Section 179 deduction previously allowed on that property.

Gift gain property. If you have capital assets, such as equipment, that you are going to sell at a profit, gift it instead. By giving it to someone in a lower tax bracket, they'll realize the same gain but pay a lower tax.

Keep loss property. Also, *do not* gift property you would sell at a loss. You're better off using the loss to offset taxable income, which is subject to higher income-tax rates.

Like-kind exchanges. In general, if you trade in your car, equipment, or real property for *"like-kind"* property, you do not immediately take into account the resultant gain or loss. The gain or loss is deferred to a later year when you sell the replacement property.

To qualify for this deferral, both properties must be business or investment property. And the properties must be similar: that is, business property traded for business property, investment property traded for investment property. Also, the properties must be of a like class. For example, real estate for real estate.

This is not something you can elect (or not). If you meet the requirements, you must defer the gain. That might not seem like a threat; however, the same applies for losses. If you have a loss and satisfy the above criteria, you cannot take the loss in the year of sale.

Therefore, if you're disposing of property with an adjusted basis greater than its fair market value, sell it. Don't gift it away or trade it in. Beware! Don't try to avoid the "non-recognition of loss" rule for like-kind exchanges by selling it to a dealer and later buying a replacement from the same dealer. If you get audited, the loss will be disallowed. Instead, sell to someone different than the person whom you're buying the replacement from.

RETIREMENT PLANS
FOR THE SELF-EMPLOYED

This section isn't for everyone. It's only for those who have enough money to put some in savings and who don't need to touch it until they're at least 59 and one-half years old. Most financial planners will advise you not to rely on Social Security alone, but to do everything you can to provide for your future.

If you can afford to put money in savings, more than likely you'll want to put it into a retirement plan. One reason is that, you will not have to pay tax on the amount you sock away in the year you sock it away. Rather, it will be included in your taxable income in the year it's withdrawn. Presumably, you will not need to withdraw it until after you're retired, and therefore it will be subject to a lower tax rate than it would have been in the year it was earned. The second advantage of putting money in a retirement plan is that the amount your retirement account earns each year will not be taxed until you withdraw it. This could amount to a good-sized nest egg by the time you retire.

Caution: Some people's tax rate might actually be *higher* after retirement. That's because of the following factors: the amount withdrawn is subject to income tax—for every dollar of income, about 85 cents of Social Security is taxable; your children might no longer qualify as dependents; and the portion of your mortgage payments that can be taken as an interest deduction might have decreased.

Rule of 72

The "Rule of 72" is used to determine how long it will take for your principal to double. You don't need to be a genius in calculus or have a fancy computer. All you need to do is divide 72 by your assumed rate of return.

For example, if you put $5000 away in your retirement plan and you earn interest at a rate of 6%, the $5000 will become $10,000 in 12 years. (72 divided by six equals 12). By comparison, if you paid taxes on that money in the year it was earned, the same $5000 could take over twenty years to reach the $10,000 level. That's because a portion of the interest earned each year gets eaten up by taxes.

An Overview

Before getting into the nitty, gritty of this topic, I want you to know that this is one of the most complex areas of our already-very-difficult-to-understand tax code. I will attempt to keep it basic, simple, easy to understand, and practical, so you can apply it to your own situation.

There are a great variety of retirement plans to choose

from. In degrees of complexity they range from the wonderfully simple to the almost-impossible-to-understand. Following is a list of many of the plans you can choose from.

- ▶ IRA (Individual Retirement Account)
- ▶ SEP plan (Simplified Employee Pension plan)
- ▶ SIMPLE (Savings Incentive Match Plan for Employees)
- ▶ MSA (Medical Savings Account)
- ▶ 401(k) plan (Deferred Compensation plan)
- ▶ Keogh plans
- ▶ CQP (Company Qualified plans)

That's a lot to choose from. However, for most self-employed business owners the IRA and/or SEP will fulfill all your retirement-plan needs. And they're simple and inexpensive to set up and to maintain. The other types of plans provide some businesses with enough additional beneficial features to warrant the extra paperwork and costs necessary to set up and operate them, but they probably aren't worth the effort to you.

▶ INDIVIDUAL RETIREMENT ACCOUNTS (IRAs)

No sweat, no hassle. Let's start off with IRAs. If you like to do things the easy way—it doesn't get any easier than this. All you have to do is go down to the bank or your investment broker and say that you want to set up an IRA. They'll give you a couple of short forms to fill out and that's that. You don't have to file anything with the IRS, and you don't need permission from your employees. Each year you just deposit up to $2,000 before your tax return is due (usually April 15).

Contribution limits. The basics are that you can make a tax-deductible contribution to your IRA each year for an amount equal to $2,000 or your earned income, whichever is less. If your business turns a profit of $40,000, you can contribute up to $2,000. If your business turns a profit of $1,500 and it's your only taxable compensation, you can contribute up to $1,500.

If you're married, whether or not your spouse is employed, you can each contribute up to $2,000 in your IRAs. However, the contribution cannot exceed your combined earned income.

▶ **TIP:** *If you do not have enough money to put into your IRA, but you will be receiving a tax refund, here's what to do. File your tax return early and claim a deduction for an IRA contribution. You do not have to make the contribution until the due date of the tax return, usually April 15. If you file early enough, you will receive the refund before the due date and you can then use that refund for your IRA deposit. Just make sure you deposit it by the original due date.*

Warning! For tax years prior to 1998, if you or your spouse were an active participant in another plan, including an SEP Plan, the amount of your tax-deductible contribution may be limited, depending on your adjusted gross income and filing status.

For tax years after 1997, the amount of your tax-deductible IRA contribution will not be affected by your spouse's active participation in another plan unless your tax returns' adjusted gross income exceeds $150,000.

The following IRA Phase-Out Charts apply for the years 1997 and 1998. The phase-out levels will increase in subsequent years.

IRA PHASE-OUT CHART for 1997

Filing Status	100% Deductible	Partially Deductible	Not Deductible
Single	Up to $25,000 MAGI	$25,000–$34,999 MAGI	$35,000 or More MAGI
Married, Filing Joint Tax Return	Up to $40,000 MAGI	$40,000–$44,999 MAGI	$50,000 or More MAGI
Married, Filing a Separate Tax Return		Up to $9,999 MAGI	$10,000 or More MAGI

Note: MAGI stands for Modified Adjusted Gross Income.

IRA PHASE-OUT CHART for 1998

Filing Status	100% Deductible	Partially Deductible	Not Deductible
Single	Up to $30,000 MAGI	$30,000–$39,999 MAGI	$40,000 or More MAGI
Married, Filing Joint Tax Return	Up to $50,000 MAGI	$50,000–$59,999 MAGI	$60,000 or More MAGI
Married, Filing a Separate Tax Return		Up to $9,999 MAGI	$10,000 or More MAGI

Note: MAGI stands for Modified Adjusted Gross Income.

▶ **HINT:** *Even if your deductible IRA contribution is limited by the above phase-out rules, it may still pay to make the full contribution. That's because the earnings on the contribution are still not taxed until the money is withdrawn. Under the "rule of 72" previously discussed, your money will still grow faster than if you put it into an account that's not tax deferred.*

Beginning in 1998, there are two new types of IRAs. One is called the Roth IRA. Your contributions into the Roth IRA are not deductible. However, the earnings on your account and your withdrawals are tax-free. So, if your contributions to your regular IRA are not deductible or do not give you a tax benefit, contribute the money into a Roth IRA instead. The other type is an Education IRA. Contributions into this type of IRA are also non-deductible. However, the distributions are tax-free as long as they are used to pay for qualified higher-education expenses.

Current year's tax benefit. The amount you put in your IRA will reduce your taxable income, subject to federal, state, and local income tax rules. However, it will not reduce your self-employment or payroll taxes. For example, if your income-tax bracket is 33% (federal 28% and state 5%), a $2,000 IRA contribution will save you $667.

Withdrawal rules. In general, monies withdrawn from IRAs will be subject both to income tax in the year withdrawn and to a 10% penalty. The penalty will not apply if, at the time of the withdrawal, any of the following applies:

▶ You're at least 59 and one-half years old
▶ You're disabled and can't do any gainful activity because of your condition

▶ *The distribution is used to pay for higher-educational expenses incurred by you, your spouse, your children or grandchildren on or after January 1, 1998.*

▶ *As of January 1, 1998, you can withdraw up to $10,000 for the purchase of a home for yourself, spouse, descendants, or ancestors, provided the purchaser is a qualified first-time home owner.*

▶ **TIP:** *There are times that IRA withdrawals that are subject to the 10% penalty will actually save you money. That's because IRA withdrawals are subject to income taxes in the year of withdrawal. By taking the money out in a year where you have no other taxable income, you might reduce the overall tax you would pay on that money.*

For example, let's say in a particular year your taxable income is reduced to zero. You decided to take a year off from work and travel the world. Or perhaps your business had a bad year and suffered a loss. In those situations, if you withdraw funds from your retirement account, even though it will be subject to the 10% penalty, you might not have to pay income tax on it. In that case it's possible that you'll have an overall tax savings—by withdrawing it in a year in which your tax rate is lower than usual.

However, before taking advantage of this, keep in mind that you might want to have this money set aside as a nest egg for your retirement years.

► The distribution was made due to your death
► The distribution was part of a series of "substantial equal periodic payments"
► The distribution is used to pay for medical expenses exceeding 7.5% of your adjusted gross income
► Certain situations where you are unemployed and the monies from the distribution are used to pay health insurance premiums

---

► **Simplified Employee Pension (SEP) PLANS**

Now, let's get into SEP plans so I can show you how to save big bucks. "SEP plan" stands for Simplified Employee Pension plan. On a rating of one to ten as to simplicity of setting-up, if the IRA is a ten, the SEP is a 9.5. It's not as simple as an IRA, but it's still easy. Just go down to your bank or investment broker and they'll show you what to do. There is a special IRS form to fill out (Form 5305-SEP), but that doesn't even need to be filed with the IRS (the bank just keeps it on file).

A SEP plan is similar to an IRA; however, it can afford you much greater tax savings. Assuming an effective federal and state income-tax rate of 33%, the maximum tax savings you can derive from an IRA is $660 (33% of $2000). Under a SEP plan, given the same tax bracket, you can save as much as $6,456. That's a huge potential difference, making it more than worth your while to explore the possibilities.

Tax benefit. The major advantage of a SEP plan over an

IRA is that you can contribute up to 15% of your employees' compensation or $30,000, whichever is less. For business owners' contributions to their own account, the limit is approximately 15% of compensation or $22,500. Compensation for owners is the profit from their sole proprietorship or partnership, or salary from their corporation. There is a very complicated formula for computing the business owner's exact limitation. Your tax preparer's software program can easily calculate your maximum contribution.

Another advantage is that you have until the due date of your business's tax return (plus extensions) to establish and fund your SEP plan. The IRA, on the other hand, must be set up and established by the original due date of your individual tax return.

Downside. The major drawback to the SEP plan is that all eligible employees must participate in the plan. So if you want to make a contribution to your SEP plan, you have to contribute the same percentage to your other eligible employees. Eligible employees are those that satisfy *all* the following requirements:

- ► 21 or older, and
- ► earn more than $400 for that year, and
- ► have worked during three out of the last five years

You can make these requirements less restrictive, but not more restrictive. For example, you can change the third requirement to one out of five years, but not four out of five years.

Prior to 1997, you were able to avoid the additional expense of funding your employee's retirement plan by setting up a SARSEP (Salary Reduction SEP Plan). Under this plan the retirement contribution was funded out of the worker's salary. It did not require the employer to make additional contributions. However, unless your company had such a plan already in place before January 1, 1997, it is not available. Instead, you might consider the SIMPLE plan discussed next.

► **THE SIMPLE PLAN**

Whenever lawmakers in Washington or the IRS announce a simplification plan related to taxes, *hold onto your wallets!* The word "simple" or any of its derivations is code for "here's another way to shift money from you to the tax industry." The SIMPLE retirement plan is not an exception to this rule.

The reporting requirements of the SIMPLE retirement plan are simpler than the very complicated Keogh and 401(k) plans. However, SIMPLE is not simpler than the SARSEP plan it replaced. According to many experts there's still far too much filing and other paperwork required for this type of retirement plan to be cost effective for most employers.

However, for certain business owners, the SIMPLE retirement plan offers more tax savings than the IRA or SEP retirement plans.

Eligibility. All employers with fewer than one hundred employees earning $5,000 or more in the previous year are eligible to provide a SIMPLE retirement plan for their employees. However, if the employer has any other retirement plan available (i.e., an SEP plan), they cannot have the SIM-PLE plan.

All employees who received at least $5,000 in the previous year and reasonably expect to receive at least that much in the current year are eligible to participate in the plan. For this purpose, self-employed individuals are considered employees. If the entity is a sole proprietorship or partnership, the owners' compensation is determined by the profit from the business.

Contributions. Under the SIMPLE plan, both the employee and the employer make contributions. The employee's contribution is a percentage (determined by the plan) of his or her wages. However, his or her contribution is limited to a maximum of $6,000 each year.

The employer may choose one of two methods to determine his or her contribution. The first method is called the "employer matching formula." Under this method, the employer matches the employee's contribution, dollar for dollar, up to 3% of the employee's compensation. The employer can choose a lower percentage; however, the percentage cannot be below 1%. Also, the lower percentage cannot be elected for more than two out of five years. In either case, the employer's maximum contribution is $6,000.

The second plan is called the "non-elective contribution formula." Under this method, the employer makes a contribution up to 2% of each eligible employee's compensation. The employer's contribution is not affected by the employee's contribution. Under this method the employer's maximum contribution per employee is $3,200.

The tax effect, contribution due dates, and withdrawal rules are the same as under the SEP plan. However, if an employee makes an early withdrawal within two years of beginning participation in the plan, the penalty is 25% instead of 10%.

Choosing Between SEP and SIMPLE

If you do not have any other eligible employees, then choose the plan that allows you to make the greater contribution. SEP is about 13.04% of your profit or salary. SIMPLE is 100% of profit or salary (up to $6,000), plus 3% of profit or salary (up to $6,000).

If you have other eligible employees, then the SIMPLE plan will generally allow you to put money in your personal retirement plan, while contributing less to your employee's retirement plans that you would be able to under a SEP plan.

▶ MEDICAL SAVINGS ACCOUNT (MSA)

The Medical Savings Account is a hybrid between a medical-reimbursement plan and a retirement plan. It allows the employer to set aside monies in a special account for each employee, including owner-employees. The monies that are deposited into this account are a deduction for the business and not taxable income to the employee. The monies will be included in the employee's taxable income in the year that they are withdrawn, unless they are used to pay for medical expenses of the employee or the employee's family. In addition, monies withdrawn prior to reaching age 65 and used for anything other than medical expenses will also be subject to a 15% penalty.

Eligibility rules. MSAs are available only to employees in businesses that satisfy *all* the following requirements.

1. Fifty or fewer employees during the current year
2. Provides employees with a high-deductible health-insurance plan
3. A deductible for individual coverage within the range of $1,500 to $2,250, and a deductible for family coverage within the range of $3,000 to $4,500
4. Does not provide any health-insurance plan other than coverage for accidents, disability, dental care, vision care, long-term Medicare supplements, or fixed payments for hospitalization
5. The self-employed business owner is not personally covered under any plan other than those excepted in #4 above

Contributions. The contribution may be made by the employer on behalf of its employees or by the employees on their own behalf. However, if the employer makes the contribution, the employees can't. Therefore, it's better for the employer to make no contribution rather than making a small one.

The maximum contribution allowed each year is as follows:

▶ For individual coverage, 65% of the policy's deductible

▶ For family coverage, 75% of the policy's deductible

Distributions. The maximum annual out-of-pocket, non-taxable reimbursable expense for each employee is $3,000 for individual coverage and $5,500 for family coverage. Non-taxable reimbursements may be made for all medical expenses that are allowed as itemized deductions. However, medical-insurance premiums are not tax-free unless they are for long-term health care, continuation coverage, or health-care coverage while unemployed.

Tax effect. Contributions made by the employer on the employees' behalf are excluded from the employees' taxable income and are deductible by the employer. Contributions made by the employees on their own behalf are deductible, as are IRA/SEPs. They're not subject to the income tax but are subject to payroll taxes. Earnings on MSA accounts are not taxable in the year earned.

Distributions for allowed out-of-pocket medical expenses are excluded from gross income. All other distributions are included in gross income. There is also a 15% penalty on all distributions other than:

- ▶ Allowed out-of-pocket medical expense reimbursements
- ▶ To an individual account holder who is at least 65 years old
- ▶ Distributions made on account of disability
- ▶ Distributions made on account of death

Did you miss the boat? If the MSA sounds like it can help you, contact your banker, stockbroker, or insurance agent to set one up. However, not all states offer the same benefits as the federal government does. Also, at the time of writing this book, the MSA was a trial program. It might

RETIREMENT PLANS AVAILABLE FOR DIFFERENT TYPES OF ENTITIES

	SEP	SIMPLE (not more than 100 employees)	MSA (not more than 50 employees)	KEOGH	CQP	401(k)
Sole Proprietorship—with no employees	Y	Y	Y	Y	N	N
Sole Proprietorship—with employees	Y	Y	Y	Y	N	Y
Partnership—with no employees	Y	Y	Y	Y	N	N
Partnership—with employees	Y	Y	Y	Y	N	Y
S Corporations—only owner-employees	Y	Y	Y	N	N	N
S Corporations—non-owner employees	Y	Y	Y	N	N	Y
C Corporations	Y	Y	Y	N	Y	Y

COMPARISON CHART

	IRA	SEP	SIMPLE	MSA	KEOGH	CQP	401(k)
Simple & Inexpensive	✓	✓					
Available Entities	Individuals	All business entities	All business entities	All business entities	All unincorporated businesses	C Corporations	All entities. However, other than C Corps, only available to non-owner-employees.
Discrimination Rules	None	Must cover all employees who are at least 21, with earnings of at least $400 during the year, and worked for you at any time during at least 3 of the past 5 years.	Must cover all employees electing to be covered and whose compensation is at least $5,000 during any 2 years preceding the plan year.		Must include all employees who are at least 21, have had at least 1 year with business, and worked 20 hours each week.	Must include all employees who are at least 21, have had at least 1 year with business, and worked 20 hours each week.	Must include all employees who are at least 21, have had at least 1 year with business, and worked 20 hours each week.

| Contribution Limitations | Lesser of $2,000 ($4,000 if married filing joint) or earned income. If you or spouse is an active participant in another plan, phase-out rules apply. | Owners: lesser of 15% or $22,500. Non-owners: lesser of 15% or $30,000. | Employee's share: lesser of 3% or $6,000. Employer's share—Matching formula: lesser of 3% or $6,000. Contribution formula: lesser of 2% or $3,200. | Individual coverage: 65% of deductible. Family coverage: 75% of deductible. | Owner: lesser of 13.04% business net income or $19,562. Non-owner: lesser of 15% compensation or $30,000. | Lesser of 25% compensation or $30,000. | Lesser of 25% of compensation or $9,240. |

not be available if you did not begin the program prior to September 1997. Consult with your adviser for more details.

> **KEOGH AND COMPANY QUALIFIED PLANS**

If under the SEP rules the number of employees you must cover would make the cost of the plan prohibitive, or if the amount of money you can sock away or the withdrawal limitations are too restrictive, you might consider the Keogh or Company Qualified plan. However, both these plans are more complicated and expensive to set up and maintain than a SEP plan. You will need professional help.

The Keogh plan is available only to sole proprietorships, partnerships, and limited-liability companies. The Company Qualified plan is available only to C Corporations. What about S Corporations? Sorry, it's SEP or nothing.

Advantages over SEP. There are three major benefits these two plans have over SEP plans:

1. Under the SEP rules, the employer must include all employees that are at least 21 years old, are earning at least $400 for that year, and have worked three out of the last five years. Under the Keogh and Company Qualified plans all employees must be covered who are at least 21 years old, have been with the business at least one year, and work at least twenty hours each week.

2. Under the SEP rules, the contributions are limited to 15% of compensation. Using the Keogh or Company Qualified plan it is possible to increase the limit to 25% of compensation.

3. The Keogh and Company Qualified plans' withdrawal rules can be more lenient.

▶ 401(K) PLANS—DEFERRED COMPENSATION PLANS

All forms of businesses can set up a 401(k) plan. These allow the employer to set up a retirement plan that is funded, either partially or entirely, out of the employees' salary. However, the plan cannot include the sole proprietor, partner, or shareholders of S Corporations. The only owners that can be covered under a 401(k) plan are C Corporation shareholders. For all other owners, if they want to be included in a plan similar to a 401(k), they have to either have had a SARSEP set up by January 1997, or use the SIMPLE plan.

Although this type of retirement plan is popular, it is generally of no value to business owners who want to personally participate in a retirement plan. Also, it is usually not economical for companies with only a few employees.

CHOOSING THE
FORM OF ENTITY
THAT'S BEST FOR YOU

There are many factors to take into consideration in deciding which form of business is right for you. There are no black-and-white answers. Many of the different factors will be discussed in this chapter, and many of these are offsetting. For example, many times I have shown clients that an S Corporation would put more money in their pockets than a sole proprietorship. But when I told them about the extra paperwork involved, they decided to forgo the money. For some, paperwork is the worst thing imaginable. For others, no matter the hassle, it's worth it if the government gets less of their money. In the end, the choice is yours.

> ### ▶ THE DIFFERENT ENTITIES

There are many different types of entities to choose from, but most of the ones you will need to choose from are discussed in this chapter. Although there are a few others, they only apply to select situations, usually involving very wealthy individuals and families. If you're in that situation, I doubt you're reading this book. Instead, you're probably paying attorneys and accountants very expensive fees to do your tax planning for you.

Sole Proprietorships—The KISS Entity

A sole proprietorship is an unincorporated business with just one owner. It's you and nobody else. You could have people working for you, but you're the only owner. I call this the *KISS* entity because it's the simplest and least expensive to set up and maintain. It is the form of choice for most business owners. More than 80% of all businesses are sole proprietors; therefore, this must be the way to go. Certainly, fifteen to twenty million business owners can't be all wrong. Or can they? We'll see.

General Partnerships

General partnerships are similar to sole proprietorships. They too are unincorporated; however, there are at least two owners. Although these are simple to organize, there are some things you should do. In most cases a partnership agreement is recommended, but not required. Also, a separate income-tax form is filed for the year. It is likely that your record-keeping costs will be more involved than in a sole proprietorship, and your tax preparations will probably be more expensive. One of the negative features of this arrangement is that each partner is bound and personally liable for the actions taken by the other partners while they are acting on behalf of the partnership. However, unlike corporations, a general partnership does have the advantages of being able to customize owners' rights to cash distributions, liquidating distributions, and tax write-offs.

Limited Partnership

A limited partnership is like a general partnership; however, at least one of the partners is a limited partner. That partner is a silent partner who is merely an investor. He or she is not active in the business, and is not liable for the negligent actions of the other partners.

Corporations

In general. In most states, a corporation comes into existence when you file Articles of Incorporation. You also need to have bylaws and to maintain corporate minutes. Like the partnership, the corporation has its own tax return, and all people who work for a corporation, even shareholders, are considered employees. Therefore, there are potentially extra forms to file, records to keep, and taxes to pay. For example, in a sole proprietorship with no employees there are no extra income-tax returns or payroll returns to file, and no extra taxes to pay. However, in a corporation, even if the sole shareholder is also the sole worker, the corporation must still file all those forms and returns and pay those payroll taxes.

One of the features of a corporation is that it is considered an entity unto itself. A sole proprietorship or partnership is treated as the alter ego of the owners. However, a corporation is considered as a completely different entity than its owners. This aspect of a corporation becomes particularly significant when we talk about limited liability.

C Corporation. This is the original form of a corporation. It also is referred to as a "regular corporation." Its main distinguishing feature is the "Inc." at the end of the business name. As a corporation, it's treated as an entity unto itself, and therefore its shareholders are not personally liable for the debts and liabilities of the corporation. Also, it files its own income-tax return and is subject to its own taxes.

S Corporation. If you incorporate your business, it will be a C Corporation unless the shareholders elect to make it an S Corporation. This is done by filing IRS Form 2253. An S Corporation is really a hybrid between a corporation and a partnership. It has the limited-liability feature of the corporation but is taxed as a partnership. This means, as you will see, the profit, loss, and other tax attributes are not taxed to the corporation but rather are passed through to its shareholders.

This form of entity is not open to everyone. The following are the requirements for a corporation to be eligible to choose to be treated as an S Corporation:

1. U.S. corporation
2. Not greater than seventy shareholders
3. No non-resident alien shareholders (however, "electing small business trusts" can own stock as of 1/1/97)
4. No corporate or partnership shareholders
5. One class of stock, but can be voting and non-voting
6. All shareholders agree, in writing, to the S status.

About 90% of all corporations elect S status. Do they know something other corporations don't? Maybe yes, maybe no.

Limited Liability Company (LLC)

This is the new kid in town (though not quite so new anymore). As an S Corporation is a hybrid between a partnership and a regular corporation, the LLC is a hybrid between a partnership and an S Corporation. It has the limited-liability feature of the S Corporation without the eligibility requirements. For instance, if one of the owners is a non-resident alien, your business can become an LLC and still be afforded the benefit of limited liability. In addition, like a partnership, it can customize owners' rights to cash distributions, liquidating distributions, and tax write-offs. These rights are not available to corporate shareholders. If you're currently a corporation, converting to an LLC may result in extra taxes. Check with your tax adviser.

Another limited-liability form of entity is the **limited liability partnership.** This entity is not available in all states. However, it is a good alternative for professional practices with multiple owners, such as attorneys and accountants. In limited liability partnerships the partners are personally protected from the negligent and malpractice actions of the other partners.

> **► CHOOSE YOUR GOAL, CHOOSE YOUR FORM**

The best way to choose the form of entity that's right for you is to match your goals with features offered by each type of entity. Listed below are the most common attributes that must be considered when determining the form of entity you should set up. After reviewing each one, decide if that's a goal that's important to you. If so, check the box to the right of the goal heading. In the next section, we will refer back to the goals we selected in helping us determine the form of entity we should choose.

1. Asset Protection ☐

This goal is relevant for people with assets. If you have nothing to protect, then you don't need protection. But if you own a house, equipment, or anything else of value, you might want to consider protecting these assets from creditors and from the liability of your company.

If your business is not able to pay its debts or liabilities then your personal assets are in jeopardy. However, there are forms of entities available where creditors of the business can go after only the assets of the business. This is called **limited liability.** This feature is an aspect of all corporations, limited liability companies, and limited liability partnerships. It is not available to sole proprietorships or partnerships.

Be careful: it is not necessarily wise to rely on insurance coverage instead of choosing a form of entity that has the limited-liability feature. Unfortunately, it's not unusual for insurance companies to go belly up themselves, leaving you holding the bag. And there's always human error. In one case, Mack owned his own truck, moving people all over the country. On one of his business trips he was away from home two months, in which time the current premium was sent to his home. He was not home to pay it on time. On his way home he was in a very bad accident. Unfortunately, his policy had lapsed just two days before. Mack was not covered. It cost him $40,000.

On the other hand, don't think that your assets are protected just because your business has limited liability. First of all, most financial institutions will require personal guarantees before lending your corporation money.

Secondly, you have to watch out for what is called "piercing the corporate veil." If you don't operate your corporation as a separate entity, it will be considered your alter ego and the limited-liability feature will not protect your personal assets. For example, every transaction between you and the company should be treated as an "arm's length transaction": your company should treat you as they would someone they didn't know. And make sure all the *I*s are dotted and the *T*s crossed.

Thirdly, you can never protect yourself from your own negligence. For instance, let us say that Tex incorporates his cab company. Joe, one of the drivers, injures a pedestrian and the insurance company doesn't pay for all the damages. Though the corporation would be liable, Tex would not be personally liable. However, in this particular case, Joe had lost his license because of five DUI (driving under the influence of liquor) incidents. Therefore, Tex was held personally liable because of his negligence in hiring Joe. Similarly, if Tex were the driver, then Tex would be personally liable.

A common mistake is having your corporation own assets, like cars. Some business owners do this under the impression that it will reduce their taxes. However, not only does it not reduce taxes, it destroys the limited-liability aspect of the corporation. Once the corporation owns the car, that asset is not protected by limited liability. In fact, it is often wise to have all your valuable assets not owned by your corporation. Have you or someone else own the assets and lease them to the company. That way, you protect the asset and, as you learned in Part Five, you will save money on taxes.

2. No Sweat, No Hassle ☐

If you're like most self-employed business owners, you're already devoting all your waking hours (and some sleeping hours) to make your business happen. And if you're running a typical start-up, you're scraping together just enough money to stay alive. In either case, the last things you might want are the red tape headaches and extra expenses. That's why most choose sole proprietorships: they abhor paperwork. And the sole proprietorship, as discussed earlier, is the easiest and cheapest entity to form and maintain.

To get started, sole proprietorship requires minimal paperwork and almost no money. All other forms of entities require separate income-tax or income information and special agreements and initial filings. And with all corporations there will be at least one employee to withhold payroll and file payroll forms for. In sole proprietorships and most partnerships, the owner-worker is not considered an employee. Whereas shareholder-workers are treated as employees for payroll-tax purposes.

3. Low Audit Risk   ☐

Nobody wants to be audited. And some people will do anything to avoid an invitation from the IRS to come visit—even not taking deductions they're entitled to. If this is your concern, read on.

As you can see from the chart below, sole proprietorships run the greatest risk of being audited. In 1993 their audit rate ranged from 2% to 4%, depending on gross receipts. In 1994 the audit range went up to 3% to 5%. And in 1995 it went up again, to 3% to 6%! On the other hand, partnerships and S Corporations hardly ever get audited. And only 1% to 3% of most C Corporations get audited. Do you get the impression that the IRS doesn't trust sole proprietors, especially those with gross receipts under $25,000?

However, don't forget one of the lessons in Part Three. Even at worst, there's only a slight chance of being audited. And even if you do get audited, you'll have nothing to worry about if you follow the audit-proofing techniques presented throughout this book. And remember, 80% of all audits result in no change, a refund, or at worst a compromise.

4. Offset Other Income with Business Loss   ☐

Most business start-ups suffer losses their first two or three years. It's not unusual to have other sources of income during those early years, so you can eat, have a roof over your head, and pay for other living expenses and the costs of starting a business without having to exhaust your savings (if you even have any). To help pay these costs, the losses from the business are used to offset the other income, which produces a much-needed tax savings. Of course, this same principle applies to all businesses, not just start-ups.

CHANCES OF BEING AUDITED

FORM OF ENTITY	1992	1993	1994
Sole Proprietorship Gross Receipts:			
Under $25,000	2.24%	4.39%	5.85%
$25,000 to Under $100,000	2.41%	3.01%	3.08%
$100,000 and Over	3.91%	3.57%	3.47%
Partnerships (*For 1994 includes LLCs)	0.61%	0.52%	*0.46%
S Corporations	1.02%	1.02%	0.46%
C Corporations Assets:			
Under $250,000	1.33%	0.84%	0.78%
$250,000 to Under $1 million	3.94%	2.47%	2.18%
$1 Million to Under $5 million	9.35%	7.11%	6.05%

Using the losses to offset income is available to all forms of entities except the C Corporation. For all other entities, the loss is passed through to the owners' personal income-tax return.

5. Take Profits Out of the Business ☐

We hope that you're in the desirable position of having to strategize in order to pay the lowest taxes on your business's profits that the law allows. Most people withdraw all the profits to pay for personal expenses, to invest, and to save. Also, taking the money out of businesses with the limited-liability feature helps protect the money if your business goes under.

As they do with business losses, most forms of entities pass through the profits to its owners. Profits are what's left over after all business expenses are paid. For corporations, salaries of shareholder-employees and officers are included as expenses.

Profits from sole proprietorships and partnerships are subject to self-employment tax and income tax at the owner's rate. Profits of an S Corporation also pass through to the shareholders; however, they are taxed as dividends and are therefore not subject to the self-employment tax.

C Corporations treat profits differently than do the other forms of entities. First, C Corporations pay a corporate tax on their profits. Second, the corporation can elect to distribute the profits to its shareholders. However, such distributions are then included in the shareholders' income and taxed at the shareholders' income-tax rate. In other words, the same dollars of income are taxed twice. This is the diabolical **double tax.**

At all costs, you want to avoid your money being taxed twice. If your company is a C Corporation, there are ways to take money out of the business without being subject to the double tax. All of the following produce deductions for the corporation and tax-free money to the shareholders:

1. Be sure to take advantage of all the methods of converting everyday living expenses into business deductions presented in Part Four.
2. Have the corporation provide its employees, especially if you and your family are the only employees, with fringe benefits. These fringe benefits include medical and dental care and retirement plans.
3. Employ the income-shifting techniques discussed in Part Five.
4. Increase your salary or give yourself a bonus at year's end. This is the least desirable, because although it's a deduction for the business, it's subject to your personal income tax and payroll taxes.

Whatever the form of entity, the best way to get money out of your business is by converting everyday living expenses or fringe benefits into business deductions. These will be deductions for the business and not taxable to you. The next best ways are the income-shifting techniques of leasing or selling assets to the business. These will be a deduction for the business. And although they are taxable to the recipient, they're not subject to self-employment or payroll taxes. Along the same lines, profits of an S Corporation are taxed as dividends to the shareholders. And since S Corporations are usually not subject to an income tax, these profits are subject only to the shareholders' personal income tax, not payroll or self-employment tax.

If you can avoid the double tax, C Corporations often offer the best opportunities to take money out of the business, tax-free. If you can't avoid the double tax and the business will have profits it can distribute to you on top of your salary, then S Corporations are a good bet. However, it will be necessary to weigh this advantage against the benefits afforded sole proprietorships that hire children under 18 (discussed in Part V), and that hire spouses (discussed in Part IV).

Words of caution. Corporations must pay their shareholder-employees *reasonable salaries*. If you avoid the double-tax pitfall of a C Corporation by increasing your salary or paying yourself a bonus, you need to be sure the total salary is not more than what someone else doing the same job would get paid. The IRS is on the lookout for C Corporations that try to avoid the double tax by paying excessive salaries. On the other hand, the IRS is also on the lookout for S Corporations that pay their shareholder-employees less than a reasonable salary in hopes of reducing payroll taxes. The following are the factors for determining the reasonableness of salary:

- ▶ Service performed
- ▶ Responsibility involved
- ▶ Time spent
- ▶ Size and complexity of business
- ▶ Prevailing economic conditions

▶ Compensation paid by comparable firms for comparable service

▶ Salary paid to company officers in prior years

6. Leave Profits in the Business   □

Believe it or not, there are times you might want to leave profits in your company. Such times are usually when you need to expand or improve your business. If this is your situation, it may pay for your company to organize as a C Corporation. Look at the charts below. As you can see, there are times that the corporate tax rate is lower than the personal tax rate.

The income ranges where the corporate tax rate is less than the personal varies depending on your filing status. For example, if in 1996 your personal filing status was single and your taxable income was $75,000, your federal income-tax bracket would have been 31% and your federal income tax would have been $18,385. The corporate tax bracket on the same taxable income was 15%, with a total tax of $13,750. If the taxpayer's status was married filing jointly, then the personal federal income tax would have been $15,787. The corporate tax remains the same, $13,750. Clearly, in either situation, it would save a lot of money to leave the profits in the business. However, in reality it is not this simple. Your personal taxable income is affected by many other factors than just your business's income—to name just a few, these would include personal exemptions, standard or itemized deductions, interest and dividends, and income from other activities.

In situations where you expect to leave profits in your

INDIVIDUAL FEDERAL INCOME-TAX RATE SCHEDULE FOR 1997

Tax Rate	Single	Married Joint	Married Separate	Head of Household
15.0%	$1–$24,650	$1–$41,200	$1–$20,600	$1–$33,050
28.0%	24,651– 59,750	40,200– 99,600	20,601– 49,800	33,051– 85,350
31.0%	59,751–124,650	99,601–151,750	49,801– 75,875	85,351–138,200
36.0%	124,651–271,050	151,751–271,050	75,876–135,525	138,201–271,050
39.6%	Over 271,050	Over 271,050	Over 135,525	Over 271,050

CORPORATE FEDERAL INCOME-TAX RATE SCHEDULE FOR 1997

Tax Rate	Corp. Taxable Income
15.0%	$1– $50,000
25.0%	50,001– 75,000
34.0%	75,001– 100,000
39.0%	100,001– 335,000
34.0%	335,001–10,000,000
35.0%	10,000,001–15,000,000
38.0%	15,000,001–18,333,333
35.0%	Over $18,333,334

business, to determine whether a C Corporation will save you money, you will need to project your total taxes, both personal and corporate, under both alternatives.

Beware of PSC! No. PSC is not a poisonous substance. However, if you're a service provider in the fields of health, law, accounting, engineering, actuarial services, performing arts, or consulting, you're probably allergic to it. If your business is one of the above service providers and it's organized as a C Corporation, there's a good chance you're a PSC (Personal Service Corporation). In that case, the corporation's profits will be taxed at a flat rate of 35%. You want to avoid this! However, if you're able to reduce the corporation's taxable income to zero, then you will be able to avoid this pitfall.

Another trap to avoid is the **accumulated earnings tax.** C Corporations that accumulate more cash than they reasonably need, instead of distributing it to shareholders, can be hit with a 39.6% tax on the excess holdings. There is a safe harbor limit of $250,000 ($150,000 for PSCs).

7. Shift Income to Lower Bracketed Taxpayers

As was discussed in detail in Part Five, there are several techniques you can employ to shift income that would be taxed at your tax bracket to others in lower tax brackets. These include hiring family members and friends, leasing equipment from others, and gifting ownership in your business. Of these, the ones that are not available to every form of entity are specifically hiring your children under 18 years old and gifting stock ownership in an S Corporation.

7-A. HIRING CHILDREN UNDER 18   ☐

By hiring your child, you shift taxable income to your child. That salary will be a deduction for your business and taxable income to your child. In effect, you are shifting income that would have been taxed at your income-tax rate, and will instead be subject to your child's income-tax bracket. And if the child is under 18 years old, the salary will be exempt from payroll taxes. In your hands, the same money would have been subject to Social Security and Medicare taxes. As you learned in Part Five, in many cases the first $6,000 you pay your under-18-year-old will be 100% tax free.

To take advantage of this great tax saver:

- ▶ the employee must be **your child,** and
- ▶ the child must be **under 18** years old, and
- ▶ your business must be a **sole proprietorship**

7-B. GIFTING S CORPORATION STOCK ☐

Earlier we discussed the advantage in payroll-tax savings from distributing profits of an S Corporation in the form of dividends. You get an additional tax-saving benefit by gifting part or all of the S Corporation's stock to individuals in a lower tax bracket than yours. This benefit does not work with C Corporations because of the double-tax issue.

Beware of the kiddie tax! This technique usually doesn't pay if the recipient is under 14 years old because of the kiddie tax. Under this tax, passive income in excess of $1,400 that is given to children under 14 is taxed at their parents' income-tax rate.

However, this method could be an advantageous way to shift income to parents who are over 65 and in a lower tax bracket than yours. The problem with shifting income to parents by hiring them is that they can receive only a certain amount of earned income before it reduces their Social Security benefits. But here you're shifting assets, not income: therefore, the income is from dividends, which is considered passive income. Since it's not earned income, the Social Security benefits are not affected.

8. Providing Fringe Benefits to Yourself and Your Family

As discussed in Part Four, the primary reason that owning your own business is considered the best tax shelter is the ability to convert everyday living expenses into business deductions. Most of those deductible expenses are available to all businesses regardless of the form of entity. However, for some, the full benefit is only available to certain forms of businesses.

8-A. MEDICAL AND DENTAL EXPENSES ☐

As discussed in Part Four, medical and dental expenses for business owners are usually not a business deduction. However, these expenses can be turned into a deduction in two situations. If the owner's business is a sole proprietorship, the owner can hire his or her spouse and provide coverage for that employee-spouse. If the spouse elects family coverage, the employee-spouse, the employee-spouse's children, and the employee-spouse's spouse (that's you, the owner) are covered. And that's a 100% business deduction!

If you are unmarried, then you can still get a 100% business deduction for medical and dental expenses if you choose the C Corporation form of entity. Of course, married shareholders can also take advantage of this benefit through a C Corporation.

Don't forget! **All** employees must be covered under a medical reimbursement plan.

8-B. TURN RETIREMENT-PLAN CONTRIBUTIONS INTO BUSINESS DEDUCTIONS ☐

Retirement plans are a great way to put money away for the future. (See Part Six for a more in-depth discussion.) The most common form of retirement plan is the IRA. The tax-saving limitations of the IRA are that the contribution is limited to $2,000 per year ($4,000 for married couples) and it only reduces the income tax, not Social Security and Medicare taxes. Most other types of retirement plans allow you to put away much more money. However, in all forms of entities except corporations, the contribution to the owner's retirement plan is not a business deduction and therefore does not reduce the owner's Social Security and

Medicare taxes. But a corporation's contribution to its owner-employee's retirement plan will effectively reduce the owner's Social Security and Medicare taxes.

By the way, the amount of contributions that you are allowed to make to retirement plans is usually based on earned income. Since dividends are not earned income, dividends distributed to you by your company do not increase the amount that you are allowed to contribute to your retirement plan.

8-C. OTHER FRINGE BENEFITS □

In general, if the following fringe benefits are provided to employees, the benefits are deductible by the employer and not taxable to the employee. However, these are only tax-free benefits to business owners of a C Corporation. Otherwise, the amount of these benefits provided to the owner is not a business deduction, and therefore is included in the owner's taxable income. Some of the more typical fringe benefits are:

- ▶ $50,000 group life insurance
- ▶ Disability insurance, including disability, wage continuation, sickness, and accident insurance
- ▶ Meals and lodging furnished on the business premises, for convenience of the employer (meals subject to 50% limitation, and lodging must be a condition of employment)
- ▶ Parking (maximum $170 each month)
- ▶ Transit passes (maximum $65 each month)
- ▶ Commuter transportion in a "commuter highway vehicle"

▶ Financial and tax planning, if part of an employee benefit plan and widely available

9. Tax-Free Loans From Business ☐

If you want to lend yourself money from your business you can, but it may cost you. If you lend yourself money from an incorporated business, you must charge yourself interest. This interest is a personal deduction to you and therefore not deductible. However, for the corporation it is taxable interest. Up to $10,000, however, the corporation's loan to a shareholder can be made without interest and is tax free.

10. Business Deduction for Charitable Contributions ☐

In general, charitable deductions are **only** deductible as a personal itemized deduction. If you don't itemize your deductions, you don't get a tax benefit from the contribution. If you do itemize, it reduces your income tax but not your Social Security and Medicare taxes. Even if your business makes the contribution, that is still not considered a business deduction. Instead it flows to you as a non-business expense.

This rule is the case for most entities, but not for C Corporations. These entities do get a deduction for charitable contributions. However, even they can only deduct up to 10% of their profit in any given year. The unused portion will be carried over to the future years.

If your C Corporation avoids the double tax by not having a taxable profit, they will not derive a benefit from any charitable contributions made during the year. And if you don't expect to show profits in the future, you may as well make the contribution personally and at least get the benefit of an itemized deduction.

11. Dividends Received for Other Corporations   ☐

C Corporations pay tax on only 30% of the dividends received from domestic corporations.

12. Raising Capital for Business   ☐

It's generally easier for a corporation to raise capital than for an unincorporated business to do so.

13. Personal Credit   ☐

When applying for personal credit, especially credit cards, you will usually find it easier to get credit if you're an employee. If you're a sole proprietor or partner, you might be asked to supply your tax returns for the last two years.

If your business is a corporation, then officially you receive a salary. In which case, you'll probably just be asked your salary. Of course they'll call your employer for confirmation!

14. Fiscal Year   ☐

In certain limited situations it's better to file your taxes on a basis other than the calendar year. Most of these situations are related to ease of bookkeeping. For instance, if you have a lot of inventory, come the end of December you may be too busy to take inventory. In that case, by choosing an alternative date to end your business year, you will be able to put off taking inventory. However, if you're not a C Corporation you will probably have to use December 31 as your year-ending date. Only a C corporation can easily choose a fiscal year.

▶ THE CHOOSING PROCESS

We all have different likes, dislikes, preferences, and phobias. Some love paying attention to details, while other shudder at even the thought. Some enjoy fitting numbers into little boxes, and others see the limitations of a box's boundary as an excuse not to conform. Some people get fulfillment out of completing forms, and others consider it a waste of their time. Deciding which form of entity to choose is often a subjective matter. Given the same situation, two people, after weighing all the factors, will often choose two different entities. Given individual preferences and the fact that there are so many factors to consider, I will not attempt to suggest what would be best for you. You need to weigh all the factors and decide for yourself.

However, as a general rule, in deciding which form of entity to choose, *first* consider the limited-liability issue. Do you have personal assets or equipment used in your business that you want to protect?

If "**yes**," you can eliminate sole proprietorship and partnership from your choice.

If "**no**," then all forms are still possible.

Once you've considered the limited-liability issue, there are no more rules of thumb. Fill out the chart below. The * next to a goal indicates something that is usually considered an important feature. Check the box in the second column if that goal applies to you. Just look back at the discussion concerning each goal on the previous pages and follow the boxes you checked there. From there on it's your choice.

▶ **N O T E :** *You're not bound to the form you now choose. As your situation changes, the form of entity that's best for you might also change. In that case, you can switch forms, usually with little, if any, limitations or adverse affects.*

To help you in your decision-making process, here are a few typical situations.

Situation #1. Starting a business. Most businesses choose to be a sole proprietorship when first starting out. This is understandable since new businesses are like newborn babies: they take all your free time and all your extra money. So you will want to devote as little time as possible to paperwork, and you will want to make sure your money is spent on the essentials necessary for survival and growth.

And as a practical matter, there might be nothing to gain by incorporating. If you don't have personal assets to protect, you need not concern yourself with limiting your liability. Also, it's likely that the tax write-offs created by converting everyday living expenses into business deductions are enough to substantially reduce your taxes. In other words, you don't need the extra deductions a C corporation offers you.

Situation #2. If you own substantial assets. Any business, start-up or not, should choose one of the types of entities that offers the limited-liability feature, if you're concerned about protecting assets.

Situation #3. Start-ups expecting business losses. If you're starting a business and you're expecting losses in the early years, you probably want to offset other (taxable) income with the losses. In that way, the resulting tax reduction is helping to finance your new venture. In this case, do not choose C Corporation, because you won't be able to pass the loss through to your personal return. If, on the other hand, your other income is low, you might not want to pass it through to your personal return. Instead, it might be more beneficial to offset taxable income from future years. In that case, it might pay to organize as a C Corporation initially.

Since most new businesses lose money during the first two or three years, many owners want both to offset their other income, and to protect their assets. In this situation, it is often best to initially organize as an S Corporation. As the business starts making a profit, convert it to a C Corporation and reduce the profit by providing more fringe benefits. The fringe benefits reduce the company's taxable income, without adding to your taxable income.

Situation #4. High medical and dental expenses. If your family's medical and dental expenses, including the cost of

ENTITY CHOOSING CHART

Goals	Applies to You	Sole Prop.	Partner-ship	LLC	S Corp	C Corp
1. Asset Protection	*			✔	✔	✔
2. Ease of Formation	*	✔				
3. Low Audit Risk			✔	✔	✔	✔
4. Offset Income with Loss	*	✔	✔	✔	✔	
5. Withdraw Profits	*	✔	✔	✔	✔	
6. Expand Business	*					✔
7. Shift Income						
A. Hire Child under 18	*	✔				
B. Gift S Corp Stock	*				✔	
8. Fringe Benefits						
A. Medical & Dental Married	*	✔				✔
Single						✔
B. Retirement Plans	*				✔	✔
C. Other	*					✔
9. Borrow from Business		✔	✔	✔	✔	✔
10. Charitable Donations						✔
11. Invest in Other Corps						✔
12. Raise Capital					✔	✔
13. Personal Credit					✔	✔
14. Fiscal Year						✔

health insurance, are relatively high, then you'll probably wand to be able to write them off as business deductions. If you're married, you can choose the sole proprietorship (if your spouse works for you as an employee) or a C Corporation. However, if you're single, you can write these expenses off only if your business is a C Corporation.

► **TAX-PLANNING STRATEGIES**

Choosing the right form of entity can be a *big* Tax Saver. And once you choose a particular form, you're not bound to it. You can change the form in accord with your ever-changing situation. The following examples illustrate how you can adjust the form to reduce your taxes.

EXAMPLES

Situation #1. Sammy purchases equipment for his new business. He purchases the equipment in his name and leases it to his business. He organizes the business as an S Corporation. By doing this, he's able to reduce his other personal income by the losses incurred from the leasing of the equipment to the corporation and by the losses incurred by the S Corporation. Also, by separating the assets from the corporation he protects them in case the business fails.

When the leasing operation starts turning a profit, Sammy gifts the equipment to family members who are over 14 years old and in a lower tax bracket than his. By doing this, the profit on the leasing of the equipment will be taxed at a lower rate. He transfers it to family members over 14 in order to avoid the kiddie tax.

When the corporation starts turning a profit, Sammy transfers stock to family members over 14 years old and in a lower tax bracket than his. Again, this reduces taxes while not falling into the kiddie-tax trap.

Situation #2. Let's say Sammy formed a C Corporation to take advantage of the extra fringe benefits. However, now the business is turning more than enough profit to cover his salary and fringe benefits. In order to avoid the double-taxation trap, Sammy splits off one of his profit centers into a second corporation. The second corporation is organized as an "S." By doing this, Sammy is able to take advantage of the C Corporation's lower tax brackets and fringe benefits. The S Corporation is used to avoid excess accumulated-earnings tax and the pitfalls of double taxation. So if your C Corporation is making a lot of money, shift one of the profit centers into an S Corporation.

Appendix A

TAX-RATE SCHEDULE FOR 1997

SINGLE INDIVIDUALS

If taxable income is:

Over	But not over	The tax rate is	Of the amount over
$ 0	$ 24,650	0 + 15.0%	$ 0
24,650	59,750	3,697.50 + 28.0%	24,650
59,750	124,650	13,525.50 + 31.0%	59,750
124,650	271,050	33,644.50 + 36.0%	124,650
271,050		86,348.50 + 39.6%	271,050

MARRIED FILING JOINT RETURNS

If taxable income is:

Over	But not over	The tax rate is	Of the amount over
$ 0	$ 41,200	$ 0 + 15.0%	$ 0
41,200	99,600	6,180.00 + 28.0%	41,200
99,600	151,750	22,532.00 + 31.0%	99,600
151,750	271,050	38,698.50 + 36.0%	151,750
271,050		81,646.50 + 39.6%	271,050

HEADS OF HOUSEHOLD

If taxable income is:

Over	But not over	The tax rate is	Of the amount over
$ 0	$ 33,050	$ 0 + 15.0%	$ 0
33,050	85,350	4,957.50 + 28.0%	33,050
85,350	138,200	19,601.60 + 31.0%	85,350
138,200	271,050	35,985.00 + 36.0%	138,200
271,050		83,811.00 + 39.6%	271,050

MARRIED FILING SEPARATE RETURNS

If taxable income is:

Over	But not over	The tax rate is	Of the amount over
$ 0	$ 20,600	$ 0 + 15.0%	$ 0
20,600	49,800	3,090.00 + 28.0%	20,600
49,800	75,875	11,266.00 + 31.0%	49,800
75,875	135,525	19,349.25 + 36.0%	75,875
135,525		40,823.25 + 39.6%	135,525

Appendix B

SAMPLE INDEPENDENT-CONTRACTOR AGREEMENT

Caution: The following sample contract is intended to give the reader an illustration of an agreement between a business and an independent contractor. It is for illustration purposes only and might not be suitable for your particular use. Before using this agreement, or any part of it, you should consult with your attorney.

AGREEMENT

Agreement is hereby made between the CLIENT and INDEPENDENT CONTRACTOR set forth below according to the following terms, conditions, and provisions:

1. IDENTITY OF CLIENT

CLIENT is identified as follows:

Full legal name of CLIENT: _____

Type of entity: ☐ Sole Proprietorship   ☐ Partnership   ☐ Corporation

☐ Other _____

Address: _____

Telephone Number: (___) ____-_____

2. IDENTITY OF INDEPENDENT CONTRACTOR

The independent contractor (hereafter ''IC'') is identified as follows:

Full legal name of IC: _____

Type of entity: ☐ Sole Proprietorship ☐ Partnership ☐ Corporation

☐ Other _____

Address _____

Telephone Number: ( )____-_____

Social Security No. or Federal E.I.N. _____

3. JOB TO BE PERFORMED

CLIENT desires that IC perform, and IC agrees to perform, the following job: _____

_____

_____

4. TERMS OF PAYMENT

CLIENT shall pay IC according to the following terms and conditions: _____

_____

5. REIMBURSEMENT OF EXPENSES

CLIENT shall not be liable to IC for any expenses paid or incurred by IC unless otherwise agreed in writing.

6. EQUIPMENT, TOOLS, MATERIALS, AND SUPPLIES

IC shall supply, at IC's sole expense, all equipment, tools, materials, and/or supplies to accomplish the job agreed to be performed.

7. FEDERAL, STATE, AND LOCAL PAYROLL TAXES

Neither federal, nor state, nor local income tax, nor payroll tax of any kind shall be withheld or paid by CLIENT on behalf of IC or the employees of IC. IC shall not be treated as an employee with respect to the services performed hereunder for federal or state tax purposes.

8. NOTICE TO IC REGARDING IC'S TAX DUTIES AND LIABILITIES

IC understands that IC is responsible to pay, according to law, IC's income tax. If IC is not a corporation, IC further understands that IC may be liable for self-employment (Social Security) tax, to be paid by IC according to law.

9. FRINGE BENEFITS

Because IC is engaged in IC's own independently established business, IC is not eligible for, and shall not participate in, any employee pension, health, or other fringe-benefit plan of the CLIENT.

10. CLIENT NOT RESPONSIBLE FOR WORKERS' COMPENSATION

No workers' compensation insurance shall be obtained by CLIENT concerning IC or the employees of IC. IC shall comply with the workers' compensation law concerning IC and the employees of IC, and shall provide to CLIENT a certificate of workers' compensation insurance.

11. TERM OF AGREEMENT

This agreement shall terminate at 11:59 p.m. on _____, 199___ .

12. TERMINATION WITHOUT CAUSE

Without cause, either party may terminate this agreement after giving 30 days prior written notice to the other of intent to terminate without cause. The parties shall deal with each other in good faith during the 30-day period after any notice of intent to terminate without cause has been given.

13. TERMINATION WITH CAUSE

With reasonable cause, either party may terminate this agreement effective immediately upon giving of written notice of termination with cause. Reasonable cause shall include:
A. Material violation of this agreement.
B. Any act exposing the other party to liability to others for personal injury or property damage.

14. NON-WAIVER

The failure of either party to exercise any of its rights under this agreement for a breach thereof shall not be deemed to be a waiver of such rights or a waiver of any subsequent breach.

15. NO AUTHORITY TO BIND CLIENT

IC has no authority to enter into contracts or agreements on behalf of CLIENT. This agreement does not create a partnership between the parties.

16. DECLARATION OF INDEPENDENT CONTRACTOR

IC declares that IC has complied with all federal, state, and local laws regarding business permits, certificates, and licenses that may be required to carry out the work to be performed under this agreement.

17. HOW NOTICE SHALL BE GIVEN

Any notice given in connection with this agreement shall be given in writing and shall be delivered either by hand to the party or by certified mail, return receipt requested, to the party at the party's address stated herein. Any party may change its address stated herein by giving notice of the change in accordance with this paragraph.

18. ASSIGNABILITY

This agreement may be assigned, in whole or in part, by IC. IC shall provide written notice to CLIENT before any such assignment.

19. CHOICE OF LAW

Any dispute under this agreement, or related to this agreement, shall be decided in accordance with the laws of the State of _____.

20. ENTIRE AGREEMENT

This is the entire agreement of the parties.

21. SEVERABILITY

If any of this agreement is held unenforceable, the rest of this agreement will nevertheless remain in full force and effect.

22. AMENDMENTS

This agreement may be supplemented, amended, or revised only in writing by agreement of the parties.

X _____   Date: _____
                XYZ Client

X _____   Date: _____
        ABC Independent Contractor

Comment: This sample independent-contractor agreement is taken from *The IRS, Independent Contractors and You!* by tax attorney—and expert in this field—James R. Urquhart III. He is a nationally recognized lecturer on the subject of independent contractors. His address is 5405 Alton Parkway, Suite A-508, Irvine, California 92604-3718, and he can be reached by telephone at 1-714-786-1170. Free employment tax resources are available at his web site located at: HTTP//workerstatus.com. Of course an agreement alone will not create an independent-contractor relationship if the factual basis is not there to support it.

Appendix C

1997 *PER DIEM* RATES (BY STATE)

(For cities and counties with a meals and incidental daily allowance rate greater than $30)

ALABAMA

Birmingham	Jefferson	38
Gulf Shores	Baldwin	34
Huntsville	Madison	34
Mobile	Mobile	38

ARIZONA

Flagstaff	All points in Cococino County not covered under Grand Canyon *per diem* area.	34
Grand Canyon	All points in the Grand Canyon National Park and Kaibab National Forest within Cococino County	38
Phoenix/Scottsdale	Maricopa	38
Prescott	Yavapai	34
Tucson	Pima County; Davis-Monthan AFB	34

CALIFORNIA

Clearlake	Lake	34
Death Valley	Inyo	42
Eureka	Humboldt	34
Fresno	Fresno	34
Gualala/Point Arena	Mendocino	42
Los Angeles	Los Angeles, Kern, Orange, and Ventura Counties; Edwards AFB; Naval Weapons Center and Ordnance Test Station, China Lake	42
Mammoth Lakes/Bridgeport	Mono	42
Merced	Merced	34
Modesto	Stanislaus	34

Monterey	Monterey	38
Napa	Napa	38
Oakland	Alameda, Contra Costa, and Marin	34
Ontario/Victorville/Barstow	San Bernadino	38
Palm Springs	Riverside	38
Palo Alto/San Jose	Santa Clara	42
Redding	Shasta	34
Sacramento	Sacramento	38
San Diego	San Diego	38
San Francisco	San Francisco	42
San Luis Obispo	San Luis Obispo	38
San Mateo/Redwood City	San Mateo	38
Santa Barbara	Santa Barbara	34
Santa Cruz	Santa Cruz	38
Santa Rosa	Sonoma	38
South Lake Tahoe	El Dorado (See also Stateline, NV)	38
Stockton	San Joaquin	34
Tahoe City	Placer	38
Visalia	Tulare	38
Yosemite Nat'l Park	Mariposa	42

COLORADO

Aspen	Pitkin	42
Boulder	Boulder	38
Denver	Denver, Adams, Arapahoe, and Jefferson	34
Durango	La Plata	34
Glenwood Springs	Garfield	34
Keystone/Silverthorne	Summit	42
Steamboat Springs	Routt	34
Telluride	San Miguel	38
Vail	Eagle	42

CONNECTICUT

Bridgeport/Danbury	Fairfield	38
New London/Groton	New London	34
Salisbury/Lakeville	Litchfield	34

DELAWARE

Dover	Kent	34
Lewes	Sussex	38
Wilmington	New Castle	38

DISTRICT OF COLUMBIA

Washington, DC	(also the cities of Alexandria, Falls Church, and Fairfax, and the counties of Arlington, Loudoun, and Fairfax in Virginia; and the counties of Montgomery and Prince Georges in Maryland) (See also Maryland and Virginia)	42

FLORIDA

Altimonte Springs	Seminole	34
Cocoa Beach	Brevard	34
Daytona Beach	Volusia	34
Fort Lauderdale	Broward	34
Fort Myers	Lee	34
Gainesville	Alachua	34
Gulf Breeze	Santa Rosa	34
Key West	Monroe	42
Miami	Dade	42
Naples	Collier	38
Orlando	Orange	34
Pensacola	Escambia	34
Punta Gorda	Charlotte	34
Saint Augustine	Saint Johns	34
Sarasota	Sarasota	34
Stuart	Martin	34
Tallahassee	Leon	34
Tampa/St. Petersburg	Hillsborough and Pinellas	38
West Palm Beach	Palm Beach	38

GEORGIA

Athens	Clarke	34
Atlanta	Clayton, DeKalb, Fulton, Cobb, and Gwinett	38
Savannah	Chatham	34

IDAHO

Boise	Ada	34
Coeur d'Alene	Kootenai	34
Idaho Falls	Booneville	34
Ketchum/Sun Valley	Blaine	38
McCall	Valley	34
Stanley	Custer	34

ILLINOIS

Champaign/Urbana	Champaign	34
Chicago	Du Page, Cook, and Lake	42
Kankakee	Kankakee	34
Peoria	Peoria	34
Rockford	Winnebago	38

INDIANA

Bloomington/Crane	Monroe and Martin	34
Carmel	Hamilton	38
Evansville	Vanderburgh	34
Indianapolis	Marion County; Fort Benjamin Harrison	38
Lafayette	Tippecanoe	34

IOWA

Cedar Rapids	Linn	34

KANSAS

Kansas City	Johnson and Wyandotte (See also Kansas City, MO)	42
Wichita	Sedgwick	34

KENTUCKY

Covington	Kenton	34
Lexington	Fayette	34
Louisville	Jefferson	38

LOUISIANA

Baton Rouge	East Baton Rouge	34
New Orleans	Parishes of Jefferson, Orleans, Plaquemines, and St. Bernard	42
Shreveport	Caddu Parish	34

MAINE

Bar Harbor	Hancock	34
Kennebunk/Sanford	York	34
Kittery	Portsmouth Naval Shipyard (See also Portsmouth, NH)	34
Portland	Cumberland	38
Rockport	Knox	34

MARYLAND

(For the counties of Montgomery and Prince Georges, see District of Columbia)

Annapolis	Anne Arundel	38
Baltimore	Baltimore and Hartford	38
Columbia	Howard	42
Frederick	Frederick	38
Grasonville	Queen Annes	34
Lexington Park/St. Inigoes/ Leonardtown	Saint Marys	34
Lusby	Calvert	34
Ocean City	Worcester	42
Saint Michaels	Talbot	38
Salisbury	Wicomico	34

MASSACHUSETTS

Andover	Essex	38
Boston	Suffolk	42
Cambridge/Lowell	Middlesex	34
Hyannis	Barnstable	38
Martha's Vineyard/Nantucket	Dukes and Nantucket	42
Pittsfield	Berkshire	34
Quincy	Norfolk	34

MICHIGAN

Detroit	Wayne	38
Gaylord	Otsego	34
Grand Rapids	Kent	34
Mackinac Island	Mackinac	38
Petosky	Emmet	34
Pontiac/Troy	Oakland	38
Port Huron	St. Clair	38
Sault Ste. Marie	Chippewa	34
St. Joseph/Benton Harbor/Niles	Berrien	34
Traverse City	Grand Traverse	34

MINNESOTA

Duluth	St. Louis	38
Minneapolis/St. Paul	Annoka, Dakota, Hennepin, and Ramsey Counties; Fort Snelling Military Reservation and Navy Astronautics Group (Detachment BRAVO), Rosemount	38

MISSISSIPPI

Biloxi/Gulfport/Pascagoula Bay/ St. Louis	Harrison, Jackson, and Hancock	34
Jackson	Hinds	34
Ridgeland	Madison	34

MISSOURI

Kansas City	Clay, Jackson, and Platte (See also Kansas City, KS)	42
Lake Ozark	Miller	34
Osage Beach	Camden	34
Springfield	Greene	34
St. Louis	St. Charles/St. Louis	42

NEBRASKA

Omaha	Douglas	34

NEVADA

Incline Village	Elko	38
Las Vegas	Clark County; Nellis AFB	38
Reno	All points in Washoe County other than the city of Incline Village	34
Stateline	Douglas (See also South Lake Tahoe, CA)	38
Conway	Carroll	34
Hanover	Grafton and Sullivan	38
Portsmouth/Newington	Rockingham County; Pease AFB (See also Kittery, ME)	34

NEW JERSEY

Atlantic City	Atlantic	38
Belle Mead	Somerset	34

Camden/Moorestown	Camden and Burlington	38
Edison	Middlesex	38
Flemington	Hunterdon	34
Freehold/Eatontown	Monmouth County; Fort Monmouth	34
Millville	Cumberland	34
Newark	Bergen, Essex, Hudson, Passaic, and Union	42
Parsippany/Dover	Morris County; Picatinny Arsenal	38
Princeton/Trenton	Mercer	38
Tom's River	Ocean	34

NEW MEXICO

Albuquerque	Bernalillo	34
Farmington	San Juan	34
Los Alamos	Los Alamos	34
Santa Fe	Santa Fe	42
Taos	Taos	34

NEW YORK

Albany	Albany	38
Batavia	Genesee	34
Binghamton	Broome	34
Buffalo	Erie	38
Corning	Steuben	34
Glen Falls	Warren	38
Kingston	Ulster	34
Lake Placid	Essex	34
Monticello	Sullivan	34
New York City	The boroughs of the Bronx, Brooklyn, Manhattan, Queens, and Staten Island; Nassau and Suffolk Counties	42
Niagara Falls	Niagara	34
Palisades/Nyack	Rockland	34
Plattsburgh	Clinton	34
Rochester	Monroe	42
Saratoga Springs	Saratoga	38
Schenectady	Schenectady	34
Syracuse	Onondaga	34
Utica	Oneida	34
White Plains	Westchester	42

NORTH CAROLINA

Asheville	Buncombe	34
Charlotte	Mecklenburg	38
Duck/Outerbanks	Dare	34
Greensboro/High Point	Guilford	34
Research Park/Raleigh/Durham/Chapel Hill	Wake, Durham, and Orange	38
Winston-Salem	Forsyth	34

OHIO

Akron	Summit	34
Cincinnati/Evendale	Hamilton and Warren	34
Cleveland	Cayahoga	38
Columbus	Franklin	34
Springfield	Clark	34
Toledo	Lucas	34

OREGON

Ashland/Medford	Jackson	38
Beaverton	Washington	38
Crater Lake/Klamath	Klamath	38
Eugene/Florence	Lane	34
Lincoln City/Newport	Lincoln	38
Portland	Multnomah	38

PENNSYLVANIA

Allentown	Lehigh	34
Chester/Radnor	Delaware	42
Gettysburg	Adams	34
Harrisburg	Dauphin	34
King of Prussia/Ft. Washington	Montgomery County; except Bala Cynwyd (See also Philadelphia, PA)	38
Lancaster	Lancaster	34
Philadelphia	Philadelphia County; city of Bala Cynwyd in Montgomery County	38
Pittsburgh	Allegheny	38
Scranton	Lackawanna	34
State College	Centre	34
Valley Forge/Malvern	Chester	38
Warminster	Bucks County; Naval Air Development Center	34
York	York	34

RHODE ISLAND

East Greenwich	Kent County; Naval Construction Battalion Center, Davisville	34
Newport/Block Island	Newport and Washington	42
Providence	Providence	42

SOUTH CAROLINA

Charleston	Charleston and Berkeley	34
Greenville	Greenville	38
Hilton Head	Beaufort	34
Myrtle Beach	Horry County; Myrtle Beach AFB	34

TENNESSEE

Gatlinburg	Sevier	34
Knoxville	Knox County; city of Oak Ridge	34
Nashville	Davidson	38

TEXAS

Austin	Travis	34
Dallas/Ft. Worth	Dallas and Tarrant	42
El Paso	El Paso	34
Galveston	Galveston	42
Houston	Harris County; L. B. Johnson Space Center and Ellington AFB	38
Lubbock	Lubbock	34
Plano	Collin	34
San Antonio	Bexar	34

UTAH

Bullfrog	Garfield	34
Park City	Summit	42
Provo	Utah	34
Salt Lake City/Ogden	Salt Lake, Weber, and Davis Counties; Dugway Proving Ground and Tooele Army Depot	38
St. George	Washington	34

VERMONT

Burlington	Chittenden	34
Manchester	Bennington	34
Middlebury	Addison	34

VIRGINIA

(For the cities of Alexandria, Fairfax, and Falls Church, and the counties of Arlington, Fairfax, and Loudoun, see District of Columbia)

Charlottesville*		42
Lynchburg*		34
Richmond*	Chesterfield and Henrico Counties; also Defense Supply Center	38
Roanoke*	Roanoke	34
Virginia Beach*	Virginia Beach (also Norfolk, Portsmouth, and Chesapeake)	38
Williamsburg*	Williamsburg (also Hampton, Newport News, York County, Naval Weapons Station, Yorktown)*	34
Wintergreen	Nelson	42

*Denotes independent cities

WASHINGTON

Anacortes/Mt. Vernon/Whidbey Island	Skagit and Island	34
Bellingham	Whatcom	34
Friday Harbor	San Juan	38
Kelso/Longview	Cowlitz	34
Lynnwood/Everett	Snohomish	34
Ocean Shores	Grays Harbor	34

Port Angeles	Clallam	34
Seattle	King	38
Spokane	Spokane	38
Vancouver	Clark	34

WEST VIRGINIA

| Wheeling | Ohio | 34 |

WISCONSIN

Brookfield	Waukesha	38
Eau Claire	Eau Claire	34
La Crosse	La Crosse	34
Lake Geneva	Walworth	34
Madison	Dane	34
Milwaukee	Milwaukee	34
Oshkosh	Winnebago	34
Racine/Kenosha	Racine and Kenosha	34
Wisconsin Dells	Columbia	38

WYOMING

| Jackson | Teton | 42 |

Appendix D

SAMPLE EMPLOYMENT CONTRACT

Caution: The following sample contract is intended to give the reader an illustration of an employment contract between a business and the business owner's spouse. It is for illustration purposes only and might not be suitable for your particular use. Before using this agreement, or any part of it, you should consult your attorney.

AGREEMENT

This agreement dated _____, 19___ is made between _____ whose address is _____, hereinafter referred to as "company," and _____ whose address is _____, hereinafter referred to as the "Employee." The company agrees to employ the employee as a _____, and the employee agrees to accept such employment in accordance with the following terms and conditions:

1. Duties of the Employee

The duties of the employee shall be: _____

2. The Employee's Work Hours

The employee's typical work hours shall be _____ hours per week. Such hours of work shall be performed during "normal" working hours, unless otherwise agreed. "Normal" working hours shall be from 9 AM to 5 PM, Monday through Friday.

3. Time Cards

The employee is required to keep a time card on a daily basis and to submit it to the company no later than _____ of the following week.

4. Compensation

The employee's compensation for work performed shall be $_____ per hour (or, a salary of $_____ per _____). The payments shall be made on the _____ day of each _____.

5. Holidays

The employee shall be entitled to the following paid holidays: _____

_____

6. Vacations

The employee will be entitled to _____ paid vacation days per year, commencing after the first 6 months of employment.

7. Health Insurance

The company shall provide suitable health insurance for the employee. Such policy shall include coverage for the employee's spouse and dependent children.

8. Medical Reimbursement

If the employee qualifies, the company agrees to include the employee in its Medical Reimbursement Plan.

9. Reimbursements

The employee shall be reimbursed for all authorized expenses incurred on behalf of the company.

10. Length of Employment

The length of employment shall be from _____ 19___ to _____ 19___.

11. Termination

Either party may terminate this agreement at any time. However, such termination must be preceded by written notice, at least 14 days prior to its effective date.

12. Complete Agreement

This agreement supersedes all prior agreements between the employee and the company and may not be modified, changed, or altered other than in writing and signed by both parties.

Both the employee and the company agree to the above terms.

_____

_____

Appendix E

RESOURCE GUIDE

Every year Congress and the IRS produce literally thousands of pages of new tax laws, regulations, and Revenue and Letter Rulings. In addition to those changes, every day the tax court and federal courts make decisions affecting the application of the tax laws. It's a full-time job just sifting through all these changes for the modifications that affect your personal tax situation.

There are many resources that attempt to help the small-business owner keep up with the ever-changing tax law. Unfortunately, since most of these resources are written for tax professionals, they contain much more information than you would ever need and are written in very technical language. The few publications that are written for the lay person are usually too glib to give you any truly useful information.

The list below contains publications and organizations that I have found to provide information that is useful to small-business owners and is written in a way that is understandable and easy to put into use. Although there are probably other resources that provide useful information and services, these are the ones with which I am familiar. If you know of others, please let me know, and I will be glad to include them in future printings and editions of this book.

NEWSLETTERS

Keep What You Earn! One-year subscription (quarterly) for $28. Two years for $48. *Keep What You Earn*, c/o Henry Aiy'm Fellman, 2888 Bluff Street,

Suite 256, Boulder, CO 80301. Ask for free trial issue at 1-800-211-0544 or Kwye@indra.com

Tax Reduction Letter. One-year subscription (monthly) for $147. *Murray Bradford's Tax Reduction Letter*, 170 Reservoir Road, San Rafael, CA 94901, 1-800-204-1907.

Tax Saving Report. One-year subscription (10 issues) included with membership in National Taxpayers Union, 108 N. Alfred Street, Alexandria, VA 22314, 1-800-829-4258.

Tax Update for Business Owners. One-year subscription (monthly) for $96. Two years for $173. Harcourt Brace Professional Publishing, Subscription Fulfillment, 6277 Sea Harbor Drive, Orlando, FL 32821, 1-800-831-7799.

ORGANIZATIONS

BIZPLAN. Provider of medical reimbursement plans. Phone 1-800-298-2923.

Keep What You Earn! Workshops on tax savings for self-employed business owners. Contact: Keep What You Earn, c/o Henry Aiy'm Fellman, 2888 Bluff Street, Suite 256, Boulder, CO 80301. Phone: 1-800-211-0544. E-mail: Kwye@indra.com

National Association for the Self-Employed. Tax research and a variety of other products and services offered to members. Contact: National Association for the Self-Employed. Phone: 1-800-232-NASE.

National Association of Tax Practitioners. This organization provides valuable information and services to professional tax preparers. Contact: National Association of Tax Practitioners, 720 Association Drive, Appleton, WI 54914. Phone: 1-800-558-3402.

National Taxpayers Union. Contact: National Taxpayers Union, 108 N. Alfred Street, Alexandria, VA 22314. Phone: 1-800-829-4258.

Tax Reduction Institute. Workshops on tax advantages for home-based businesses. Contact: Tax Reduction Institute, 13200 Executive Park Terrace, Germantown, MD 20874. Phone: 1-800-874-0829.

James R. Urquhart III. Mr. Urquhart, a tax attorney and expert on the subject of independent contractors, and author of *The IRS, Independent Contractors and You!*, publishes a monthly newsletter entitled "The Independent Contractor Report." For more information, he can be contacted at 5405 Alton Parkway, Suite A-508, Irvine, CA 92604. Phone: 1-714-786-1170.

IRS PUBLICATIONS

The Internal Revenue Service provides many free publications related to tax matters. Below is a list of many of the IRS publications that you might find relevant to tax issues concerning your business. Bear in mind that although these publications can supply you with basic tax information, they are often difficult to understand well enough to apply to your situation. Also, they only inform you of the IRS's position; they will not tell you about possible alternative approaches that will save you money, or let you know about conflicting court rulings. Use these publications with the understanding that you will learn only the basic tax law, not tax-saving strategies. To order IRS publications call 1-800-TAX-FORM.

PUB#

17	Your Federal Income Tax (For Individuals)
334	Tax Guide for Small Business
509	Tax Calendar
483	Travel, Entertainment, Gift, and Car Expenses
501	Exemptions, Standard Deduction, and Filing Information
502	Medical and Dental Expenses
523	Selling Your Home
533	Self-Employment Tax
537	Installment Sales
541	Partnerships
542	Tax Information of Corporations
544	Sales and Other Dispositions of Assets
580	Retirement Plans for the Self-Employed
583	Starting a Business and Keeping Records
587	Business Use of Your Home
589	Tax Information on S Corporations
590	Individual Retirement Arrangements
911	Direct Sellers
929	Tax Rules for Children and Dependents
946	How To Depreciate Property
1542	*Per Diem* Rates

INDEX

About the Author

HENRY AIY'M FELLMAN lives in Boulder, Colorado. He has served small businesses as an attorney, accountant, and financial adviser for more than twenty years. His expertise is taxation, especially as it relates to the self-employed.

Henry Aiy'm Fellman attended undergraduate school at the University of Bridgeport, where he majored in accounting. After graduating in 1972, he entered Brooklyn Law School and received his Juris Doctor in 1975. He has practiced law in Colorado, New Mexico, Arizona, and New York. After working in the tax law department of one of the nation's top CPA firms, he started his own private practice, which he has had for the past eighteen years.

In 1995 he founded Keep What You Earn!™, an organization dedicated to teaching small-business owners how to keep more of their hard-earned money. His workshops and tax-update newsletters are offered throughout the country. He has taught and lectured at various schools and associations, such as the University of Colorado, Boulder, Graduate College, the Economic Institute, Boulder Chamber of Commerce, Colorado Free University, Life Long Learning, The Learning Exchange, Colorado Independent Publishers Association, the Rocky Mountain Translators Association, Win/Win, Rocky Mountain Inventors Congress, and Barnes Business School.

He cohosted a radio talk show, was a guest on more than fifty radio shows, and has written numerous articles and publications on taxes and business-related topics. Four times each year he publishes a newsletter informing readers of the latest changes in the tax law and the newest tax-saving ideas.

Henry can be reached at 1-800-211-0544, 1-303-782-6571, or Kwye@indra.com

Here's the information about my workshops:

KEEP WHAT YOU EARN!™
Workshops

Henry Aiy'm Fellman, through his organization Keep What Your Earn!™, presents workshops throughout the country. These workshops are designed for self-employed business owners, service providers, entrepreneurs, home-based businesses, and contractors who want to keep more of their hard-earned money. By the end of the workshop you will learn how to reduce your taxes and audit-proof your tax return. By the end of the workshop, you'll be surprised how easy the concepts are to understand and how simple the techniques are to put into action. And, what's more, you'll have fun.

These workshops are presented throughout the country. Please contact us if the members of your organization, association, or group are interested in a Keep What You Earn!™ Workshop designed specifically for their needs, or if you are interested in attending a Keep What You Earn!™ workshop in your area.

CALL:
1-800-211-0544

WRITE:
Keep What You Earn!
2888 Bluff Street, Suite 256
Boulder, CO 80301